To Jean,

Best wishes for the Christmas Season!

Love,

Gisela and George
November 2007

In God's Hands

A Nobelwoman's Struggle for Survival in War and Revolution

Ellen von zur Muehlen

Commentary by her Daughter

Gisela v. z. M. Ives

In God's Hands:

A Nobelwoman's Struggle for Survival in War and Revolution

Published by Warren Publishing, Inc.
www.Warrenpublishing.net

ISBN 1-886057-37-1
Library of Congress Catalog Number : 2007933741

Printed in the United States of America
First Edition
Cornelius, North Carolina 28031

In memory of Mamutschka

and in honor of my husband George,

and our wonderful children,

Caroline, Tanya, Toby and Allen,

and our equally wonderful grandchildren,

Joseph, Mary Ellen, George IV, and Jane

GI

CONTENTS

ACKNOWLEDGEMENTS

Mother originally wrote her memoir in German back in the 1970s. It was initially translated by her granddaughter, my sister's child, Iris Mendels, who is fluent in English and German, as well as French. Iris was very close to Mamutschka and did a superb job of translation with a deep feeling and understanding for the subject matter.

The publication of this book would not have been possible without the hard work over a number of years by my husband, George, both in putting it together on the word processor and in further editing the English text. He and mother worked together until her death in 1985, adding descriptive passages to material that George thought needed further development. He continued editing the manuscript over the intervening years until just before publication. We wrote together my commentary that has been added to the original text, he carefully molding together my and his own thoughts about how the narrative should read.

In addition, there have been many dear friends who took an interest in the eventual publication of this memoir and who have given us constructive suggestions and encouragement over the years. We want to thank all of the following: Kaye Anne and Bill Aikins, Jane Ann and

Nick Blackerby and their son Brit Blackerby, Paddy and Dan Blalock, Christian and Jack Cobb, Julia and Frank Daniels, Frankie and Pete DuBose, my sister-in-law Katherine Ives Gheesling, Bobbi and Harry Jacobs, Jane Millns and her son Robby Millns, Miriam and Henry Nicholson, Elsie and Baxter Sapp, Jane Slick, Rollie Tillman, Martha Uzzle, Joy and Charles Whitman, and Fran Young. In England, my cousins Posy Stockman, Jane Annis and Peter Scott filled in some family information that was missing, as did in Germany my cousins Hasso von Samson-Himmelstjerna and Patrik von zur Mühlen.

Finally, George and I want to particularly thank Cathy Brophy and all the good people at Warren Publishing, especially copy editor Jere Armen who helped us keep our syntax straight. It has been a pleasure working with this talented group.

FAMILY TREES

VON SAMSON-HIMMELSTJERNA

VON ZUR MÜHLEN

von Samson-Himmelstjerna

VON SAMSON-HIMMELSTJERNA

HOUSE OF HUMMELSHOF

NIKOLAI
(1828-1869)

AXEL = JENNY von STRYK
(1861-1950)   (1868-1945)

IRENE   = THEODOR BARON von der OSTEN-SACKEN   MADELEINE = RALPH MONTAGU-SCOTT
(1887-1982)   (1876-1965)   (1888-1958)   (1878- 19 ?)

NANUSCHKA   LJUBA   MICHAEL   DUNSTAN
(1913-2005)   (1914-199?)   (1910- 19 ?)   (1911-1998)

NIKOLAI   ELLEN   = MAX von zur MÜHLEN   OTTOKAR   GABRIELE
(1890-1890)   (1892-1985)   (1888-1946)   (1893-1917)   (1896-1956)

ILSE   LJUBA   IRIS   HERBERT   GISELA
(1918-2002)   (1920-1921)   (1920-1921)   (1922-1944)   (1931-)

JENNY   =   WILHEM von CRAMER   REMBERT = SYBIL BRUMBY EDWARDS
(1898-1985)   (1879-1945)   (1900-1979)   (1914-1994)

HEINZ
(1924-)

zur Mühlen
W 1792

VON ZUR MÜHLEN

HOUSE OF WOISECK

MORITZ
(1812-1883)

LEO = ANNA von MÜHLENDAHL
(1854-1942)   (1853-1942)

VICTOR = 1. HERMINE COUNTESS FOLLIOT de CRENNVILLE-POUTET   EGOLF = MARIA BARONESS von der TAUBE
(1879-1950)   (1883-1951)
          2. BIRUTTA EICHEN   (1881-1942)   (1885-1928)
             (1914-1945)

ARVED = 1. LUDOVIKA COUNTESS von KELLER   MORITZ = 1. NORA von DEHN
(1883-1945)   (1885-1965)   (1885-1945)   (1902-?)
         2. NORA von DAMNITZ   2. HELENE BARONESS von FERSEN
            (1893-1980)   (1913-1998)

MAX   =   1. ELLEN von SAMSON- HIMMELSTJERNA
(1888-1946)   (1892-1985)
               2. MARGARETHE von SOKOLOWSKI
                  (1895-1958)

ILSE   LJUBA   IRIS   HERBERT   GISELA
(1918-2002)   (1920-1921)   (1920-1921)   (1922-1944)   (1931-)

ILSE = 1. ALFRED COUNT RACZYNSKI   NELLY = ROLF von OETTINGEN
(1893-1945)   (1881-1947)   (1895-1938)   (1891-1962)
        2. GEORG von DEHN
           (1904-1945)

Ellen von zur Muehlen

EUROPE: THE BALTIC STATES

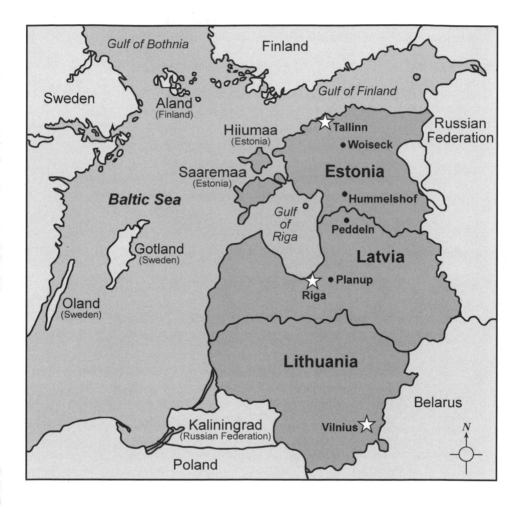

INTRODUCTION

My mother, Ellen von Samson-Himmelstjerna von zur Muehlen (her children and grandchildren came affectionately to call her *Mamutschka,* which means "little mother" in Russian), had written her memoirs before her death in 1985. Born in 1892 on her father's estate, Hummelshof, in Estonia, she describes how a large working estate was managed and the grand but formal and disciplined lifestyle that was typical of the Baltic German nobility at that time and place. But their world was turned upside down in the aftermath of World War I and the Bolshevik Revolution in Russia. My mother tells the story of her fight for survival during this period and again during World War II in our flight from the Soviets, ending in the burning ruins of Berlin during the last days of the war. In my father's family, five siblings out of seven had been murdered by the Soviets by the end of World War II or soon after.

From the 13th century, for nearly seven hundred years, the Baltic Germans constituted the landed and ruling class in the region of contemporary Estonia and Latvia. Germans had come to the area as traders and Christian (Catholic) crusaders. During the 16th century, the Lutheran Reformation took hold in Estonia and Latvia, while Lithuania remained largely Catholic. This religious development was facilitated by immigrating German Lutheran pastors, whose presence became an important part of life on the somewhat isolated Baltic German estates.

From these beginnings, the Baltic Germans settled over much of the countryside, developing their landholdings while at the same time gaining political, cultural and economic dominance. This dominance lasted throughout the centuries more or less intact, in spite of invasions through the years alternately by mostly Swedish or Russian forces. In the early 18th century Russian Tsar Peter the Great completed the incorporation of the Baltic provinces into the Russian Empire while at the same time guaranteeing the position of the ruling Baltic elite.

A reversal of fortune for the Balts began in the 1860s with a demand from Russian nationalists for greater Russification and political control of the area by Tsarist Russia. Another factor affecting the position of the Baltic Germans was the growing and understandable national movement among Latvians and Estonians for greater inclusion in the political and economic system.

By the beginning of the 20th century, about 1100 of these large manor estates accounted for 42% of the arable land in Estonia, while some 70,000 small farmsteads shared the rest. The division of land in Latvia was similar. By this time dairy and cattle had replaced grain as the main products on the estates, with the principal consumer being Russia. The Baltic provinces also acted as a breeding station for pedigree cattle and horses.

The Baltic Germans were efficient managers of their estates, many having been trained in the natural sciences or agronomy at Dorpat

University (now Tartu) in Estonia or in Germany. For example, my father, Max von zur Mühlen, after his university studies at Dorpat, received further post graduate training in forestry in Germany. Before the Latvian expropriation after World War I, his estate, Planup, where I was born in 1931, contained almost 5,000 acres of good timber land.

The 1905 revolt in Russia, which was precipitated by the Russo-Japanese War and the defeat of Russia therein, stirred already troubled waters. Some of the Baltic manor homes were destroyed and their occupants murdered by revolutionaries during this period, but the revolt was soon put down by Tsarist forces. When World War I began in August 1914, almost all Baltic Germans of military age were to serve as Russian imperial officers, though the Russian authorities became increasingly suspicious of possible collaboration between them and the German enemy. Many of the young sons of the Baltic German nobility, including my father and his brothers, completed honorary service in the Life Guards of Tsarina Alexandra, who herself was German-born and a cousin of Wilhelm II, both of whom were grandchildren of Queen Victoria of England.

After the Bolshevik Revolution in 1917, the three Baltic provinces of Tsarist Russia became independent, democratic, but socialist republics. The vast land holdings of the Baltic Germans were confiscated, typically leaving the manor house and a relatively small surrounding plot of land. Many of the Balts of my grandparents' generation emigrated to Germany or Sweden where they had cultural and/or family ties, while most of the younger generation, such as my parents, stayed behind to make a living as best they could.

What follows is my mother's story, in her own words, of her life-long struggle to stay alive and protect her family, when the privileged world into which she was born was swept away by war and revolution. Where indicated, I have supplemented her narrative with my own commentary on these events, through both my own recollection and subsequent conversations with other family members. My mother's narrative will be in plain text and mine in italics type.

Gisela Ives

Durham, North Carolina

1. Hummelshof

As I look back on my childhood days, I realize now that the strict discipline of my upbringing served me well during later years of upheaval, when our way of life disappeared forever in the aftermath of war and revolution. I was born at Hummelshof on the estate of my father, Axel von Samson-Himmelstjerna, on April 7, 1892. We had two other estates in the area, Assikas and Adscher, all of which were located in the Baltic provinces of Tsarist Russia (now Estonia). We were Baltic Germans of European nobility, as our forefathers had come from many parts of Europe besides Germany—particularly Sweden and France. In our everyday life we spoke principally German, but my parents and later we children were required to learn Russian and also French and English, as well as the language of the Baltic province in which we lived (Estonian and later Latvian).

Hummelshof was a large estate, as were many of the Baltic German landholdings, specializing in forestry, dairy farming and horse breeding. My father also had established a fresh-water area for breeding trout. All of Hummelshof's products enjoyed a fine reputation in the surrounding markets and in St. Petersburg. I was told that even Tsar Nicholas and his family were familiar with and purchased the products of the estate.

The work of the estate required many employees. For example, there were a number of German-trained foresters and their assistants.

The dairy farm and buttery were managed by a sizeable staff to look after the approximately three hundred milk cows and their calves. There were also sheep, pigs and hundreds of chickens and turkeys requiring attention, as well as thoroughbred and work horses for riding and carriages. We had an enormous fruit and vegetable garden and greenhouse. The head gardener, who was excellent at his work, had many helpers. Their produce was consumed mainly on the estate to help feed the family and the house employees. In addition to their wages, the estate field workers lived in village-like housing located on and provided by the estate, with their own gardens and animals. In many instances the workers were second and third generation employees whose parents and grandparents had worked for my father's forebears. There was a strong feeling of mutual respect and caring between the family and our employees.

The main house where I was born was a very old and large, brick country house with a high tower on one side. From the tower, a flag was always flown bearing our family colors when my father was at home. The house had three stories (plus a large basement), comprising around forty rooms with servants' quarters and bedrooms for the family and the many guests who were often visiting. The downstairs had a number of very large and high-ceilinged rooms. The dining room could seat around thirty people, with several adjoining salons for gathering before dinner. There was also a ballroom which could accommodate a large number of guests for festive occasions.

The household staff consisted of a butler and one footman (more were added when needed); a cook and helpers to attend to the three dining rooms (two for the servants); a number of household maids, including a personal maid for my mother and one for us children; and finally nannies when we were young children. For transportation there were a coachman and several stable boys who looked after the horses and carriages. Later on my father added an automobile and chauffeur to the household.

There was no electricity on the estate (but there was a telephone), and therefore the rooms were lighted with petroleum lamps and candles. The house was heated by fireplaces and large tile ovens in each room for burning wood. These ovens would remain hot for several days and were quite functional, considering the bitterly cold winters and the large, high-ceilinged rooms.

My father was the district commissioner of the large county of Fellin, where we lived. He was for this reason a very busy man and frequently had to travel. My mother married my father when she was only seventeen years old. It must have been very difficult, being so young, to manage the household of such a vast estate. Perhaps this was the reason why she became a hard, cold, and strict person.

We were eight brothers and sisters. Two of my brothers died, leaving five sisters and one brother, who was also the youngest. Our first years of life were spent under the care of nannies. I remember mainly the playroom, which had large windows reaching from the floor to the ceiling. I often sat by the window and spent many hours looking out. I remember one unforgettable scene as I was sitting there one day when two of our dogs, the borzoi, Sakol, and the Newfoundland, Caesar, jumped a deer that had wandered into the heavily snow-covered park, and in its confused fright, had approached the house too closely.

I also still see before my eyes my brother Ottokar, who was one year younger than I, as he scraped a larger and larger hole into the wall with his little fingers, eating the plaster. I was told later that he had had rickets. At that time there was no known cure for this disease. No doubt today it is no problem. He had been an angelic, beautiful child, with white-blond locks and large blue eyes. He died of dysentery in 1917, and was thus spared the upheaval in our lives.

Two of my early childhood summers are still vivid in my memory. We spent them in the care of Aunt Juli at the coastal resort of Pernau on the Baltic Sea. She was an entirely different person from those we were usually with, and her lifestyle was quite carefree. I must have been five years old. I was very happy there, because I had the first opportunity to play with other children. Although I was the youngest and the only girl, I followed a group of boys, because I especially loved their playing "wild Indians" in the park. They wanted me to be their squaw, stay in the tent, and pretend to cook for them. But I wanted to be an Indian warrior, too!

These boys were all the children of family acquaintances. But I also had other friends who did not look very pretty, who were dirty and poorly dressed, but who had my deepest admiration because they were able to do something which, in spite of much practice, I could not accomplish: they could spit amazingly far, hardly moving the mouth. Once, when I was sitting with them at the edge of a ditch practicing, an elegant carriage pulled by four snow-white horses passed by. In it sat one of my aunts. She looked at me with horror as she drove past and shook her finger reprovingly at me. I felt very ashamed, but in spite of that I did not want to give up my friends.

One of my greatest joys during these summers at my aunt's place was the daily swim in the ocean. A thick rope limited the area where small children were allowed to swim. We had buckets, shovels, and cake forms, and we built castles and deep ditches, which slowly filled with water.

One day I was invited to the birthday party of my friend Nicko, who was about eight years old. At the end of the party a photographer came to take a group picture. Nicko sat in the middle on a chair with a wreath around it, surrounded by all the boys. As his best friend, he asked me to stand beside him. I was permitted to hold his little porcelain dog, but I was warned to be careful not to let it fall because it was his favorite toy. However, to my great despair, the dog slipped out of my hand, fell on the floor, and one of the legs broke off. Nicko and his mother came right away to console me and assured me that the leg could be glued on and that the damage would no longer be visible. But I was devastated to have broken Nicko's favorite toy, and the incident haunted me for a long time.

When we returned again to Hummelshof, a big surprise was waiting for us: a light grey, three-year-old, large pony with Arab blood and a lively temperament. It was named Hopsassa, which suited it well, for the name in German slang indicates running and jumping. How my two sisters Madeleine and Irene, who were four and five years older than I, managed to ride Hopsassa, I do not know. In any case, I was always thrown off and the horse ran away. In order to prevent this, our footman, Ferdi, was told to ride a horse holding Hopsassa on a line. He was not a great horseback rider either, and I still see him before me as he fell from his horse, throwing up his arms and screaming, "My God, my God!" Hopsassa right away used the opportunity to rid herself of me and, kicking several times, took off. However, it was not very long until I managed to handle Hopsassa by myself. Two other ponies, named Grauchen and Umma, were acquired for us children. This way, my two sisters and I could go riding together. The riding path led through our five-kilometer-long park, following the river and then continuing into the forest.

2. Mali

One of the tasks of our nanny, Mali, was to soap us in the evening and then shower us with cold water. We underwent this each time with shivers and trembling. It was especially unpleasant in the winter when the water was ice cold. An acquaintance had advised my mother to have this done because it was a good means of hardening us. This may have been true, for we were practically never sick. It has become a habit for me and I continued to do it into my old age, although now I prefer to take hot baths as well.

After we were in bed, Mali used to collect some of our clothes, sit at the window, and darn and sew until all was mended. While she worked, she sang with a monotonous voice, always the same song. It still resounds in my ears. The words were as follows:

"Where could my sweetheart be?

He is not here, he is not there.

He must be in America!"

Almost asleep, I sadly thought of Mali, who could not find her sweetheart.

3. My Father

My father was fond of talking about Tsar Alexander I, whom he greatly admired. He frequently told anecdotes about him. Everything my father told us about the Tsar deeply impressed me. He reigned from 1801 to 1825, and attempted without success to bring liberal reforms to Russia. He was the favorite grandson of the Empress Catherine the Great. His educator and tutor, a liberal Swiss, exercised great influence over him. After the murder of his father, the feeble-minded Paul I, he unwillingly became Tsar of all Russia. It is said that he often cried out in despair, "I am Tsar and sole ruler of the land, and I do not even have the power to enact a single reform!" For political reasons he was also forced to marry a princess he did not care for.

The Tsar continued his attempts to introduce reforms without success. It is said that within his mind the Tsar slowly developed a plan to escape his role as ruler. He detested being Tsar, and his younger brother had agreed to sit on the throne in case of Alexander's death. One of the Tsar's soldiers resembled him so much that he had been used on occasion as a double. One day this soldier became very ill and had only a short time to live. Tsar Alexander ordered that the soldier be secretly brought to the Crimea, where he was cared for. Meanwhile he let spread the news that the Tsar was ill, and was on his way to the Crimea, accompanied by the Tsarina, in order to recuperate. He decided to live in a small, isolated house, rather than one of the palaces, and only a few faithful servants remained with him. The soldier was brought secretly to the house and put in the Tsar's bed. The Tsarina, according to custom, was obliged to sit beside the bed of the dying "Tsar." A bulletin broadcast his serious illness. When the soldier died, he was buried as Tsar with much pomp and honor. The Russian people, however, did not believe in the death of their beloved ruler. It was rumored that he was alive, but his whereabouts was unknown, and they hoped for his return. It was said that one night a tall, slender monk, enrobed in a cowl, left the Tsar's house. (The Tsar was tall and slender, with handsome facial features.) He walked to the edge of the Black Sea where a boat was waiting for him. He stepped into the boat and was rowed to a ship anchored nearby.

After a lengthy interval, the rumor spread that deep in the forest near Finland there lived a hermit in a small hut. People sought out this hermit and asked counsel of him. His advice was intelligent and wise, and more and more people made the pilgrimage to his hut. Those who visited him became convinced that this hermit was Tsar Alexander. But one day the hut was found empty. The hermit had left it forever. Later it was rumored that the Tsar had been seen in a train to Siberia. But for a long time after, nothing was heard of him. Then a new rumor started about a hermit living deep in the woods of Siberia. Again people came to visit him and ask his advice. His wisdom and goodness were widely praised. People came from everywhere in masses, because this time again they believed it was Tsar Alexander. After some time, the hermit disappeared again. Never again was anything heard from Tsar Alexander. It was generally believed that he found refuge in a monastery. But still, for many years, people hoped for his return.

While telling wonderful stories, my father did not enjoy sitting idle. He therefore got the idea to make a Gobelin (needlepoint) wall hanging for each of his daughters. Our carpenter made a large, wooden frame for my father; each carpet was to be three meters long and two meters wide. My father used very thick wool in the most beautiful colors. For each one of his five daughters, he chose a different cultural theme and worked on each for three years.

Mine had a Baroque pattern and was exquisitely beautiful. I loved and valued this carpet as something irreplaceable and used it only as a wall hanging. No one was to walk on it. Amazingly, I was able to save the rug through many flights as a refugee later in my life, but in the end I had to leave it behind when we were forced to flee on foot and everything had to be left.

I can still see my tall father as he bent over his work, which was stretched on its enormous frame, as he stitched and stitched. He was otherwise also a very busy man, being district commissioner and owner of several large estates. To work on the carpets must have helped calm his nerves. I remember my father only as a good and friendly person; I can still hear his laughter. Unfortunately our misguided upbringing, although normal for the times among the upper classes, kept us since infancy distant from our parents. Not until I was already a grandmother and my father was a very old man did I have the opportunity to discover his true, generous nature and felt able to turn to him in complete confidence. He helped me with advice and decisions in difficult times, which I could not have handled alone.

4. My Father's Birthday

The birthday of my father, on the 29th of October, was celebrated every year with incredible pomp and lasted three days. Each day began with a drive-hunt and ended with a large banquet and a ball. The gentlemen from nearby estates and some further away came accompanied by their ladies, usually with their own horses and carriages. Other guests were picked up at the railway station with our carriages. In the days leading up to this event, big preparations were made, especially by the cook and his staff. The butler with his helpers also worked feverishly. All the guestrooms were prepared by the maids and our gardener brought masses of flowers from the greenhouse. Then the first guests arrived. Those who lived further away arrived the day before the first hunt, and others arrived early in the morning of the first day.

After a hearty breakfast, everyone went into the forest. A long row of beaters under the supervision of the game-keeper had to chase the game toward the hunters who had positioned themselves in the forest. At noon lunch was brought by the butler to one of the game-keeper's houses where he set a long table with his helpers. The tired, frozen and hungry hunters were happy to have a warm meal. Not before evening did the hunters return to the house.

After a rest for everyone, the evening banquet began. The ladies appeared in full evening dress and the men in tailcoat with white tie. Each couple first went in to the *zakuska* ("appetizer") room which was next to the large dining room. In the middle of the room, arranged on a long table, were beautifully decorated appetizers, including the ever-present caviar. This was accompanied by several types of vodka. It was drunk out of special small glasses and had to be swallowed in one shot for best effect. In our area the custom prevailed that the men served the food to the ladies and inquired after their wishes. After the *zakuski* everyone went into the dining room. The dinner began with a clear, delicious bouillon soup, with which *pirozhky* were served—small turnovers with savory fillings. Usually there were seven courses. With each new course a different wine was served, and with the cake, champagne. At the end, fruit was passed around and various types of cheeses, with butter, white and pumpernickel bread. After the dinner had ended, the guests dispersed into various small salons where coffee was served in demitasse, accompanied by a choice of liqueurs. In the large ballroom couples were dancing.

We children, however, had to remain in the rooms on the upper floor, and we were not allowed to appear. All the employees were busy downstairs. Even Mali, after she had prepared our dinner, rushed back downstairs. We felt free and full of adventure. Once, after the guests had left the dining room, we quickly ran down the stairs to the dining room table. There we drank all the leftover wine in the glasses. This gave us a wild desire to romp about. Without a noise we went back up the stairs to our room. One of us took the burning oil lamp from the table and placed it on the floor. Then we all danced wildly around the lamp. Fortunately, Mali heard the noise, and I can still see her horrified expression as she entered the room. She put the lamp back on the table and sternly warned us to calm down and be quiet.

Once we had reached the age of sixteen or seventeen we were allowed to participate in the festivities. My two older sisters were permitted to join long before me. I still had to wait a few years. Yet, in time, my turn came. My braids were changed into a chignon which was fastened with hair pins. The silk ball dress reached to my toes and the matching silk shoes appeared to me to be very elegant. I now had to greet the guests. I kissed the hands of the elderly ladies, and the gentlemen bowed their heads before me. It was difficult for me not to respond with the habitual curtsy which was required of children, and I was not always successful. The dancing I liked best. I could have danced the whole night through. But let us return to my childhood.

5. The Fire in the Stables

In order to recount a terrible and unforgettable experience, I must first set the background. We had a large and long stable seven minutes away from the house. It was a sizeable complex of buildings whose view was hidden from the house by large trees, except in the winter. In the stable two hundred beautiful Angler milk cows were kept, plus six large and mean bulls. There were also about seventy calves, ten horses and a herd of sheep. Adjoining the animal stable, separated by a large wing door, was the fodder barn filled with straw and hay. Adjoining the barn was the pig stable housing about thirty pigs, and next to this was another giant barn also filled with straw, hay and other things. These buildings stood together forming a square in the middle of which there was the dung heap. This was also the place where the bulls were allowed to roam. I watched them at times as they fought with each other violently, but, since they were equally strong, they could not hurt each other.

My mother was the one who managed the cattle and the dairy. The large dairy building stood next to the cattle stable and was taken care of by the dairy farmer and his assistants. The dairy farm had to process about seven hundred gallons of milk daily. This included the milk of about one hundred additional milk cows from the neighboring estates, Assikas and Adscher. The feeding and cleaning of the animals was taken care of by the "feeding master" and his assistants. The cows were milked three times a day by about fifteen to twenty people. Cleanliness was strict; the workers had to wash their hands and each cow's udder before milking every cow. The milk was poured through a sieve and several layers of cheesecloth into the milk cans. These were then stored in a cool place. Very early every morning several horse-drawn wagons brought the milk to the railroad station, about thirteen kilometers away. From there the milk was transported by train to St. Petersburg, where it always arrived fresh. All this was organized by my mother. Her pride in her accomplishment was very justified, because it was well known that Hummelshof was one of the best-managed landed estates in the Baltics.

But back to my story. It was a cold night in January, and deep snow covered the ground. My sister and I said good night to our parents and, as usual, at nine o'clock went upstairs to our bedrooms. Immediately we noticed a tremendous flaming column coming from one end of the pig stable. We screamed with terror and raced down the steps to tell our parents. My father immediately called the fire station which was many kilometers away, but, with tired horses and deep snow, they arrived much too late. Our own small firehouse was useless except to wet down the surrounding roofs to prevent the fire from spreading.

People came running from all directions to attempt to save the animals. All the horses could be led out of the stable, yet a few, wild with fear, ran back into the burning building. The cows and bulls had tangled themselves in panic in their chains and they could not be freed, except for one bull and thirty cows. They were the only ones whose lives could be saved. The stable was now filled with smoke and the animals were lying suffocated on the ground. Nobody dared to go into the stable any more. At this point our footman, Ferdi, and the gardener, Ronk, noticed that my father must still be in the stable, for no one had noticed him coming out. Immediately they decided to enter the stable once more to search for him. They ran down the long stable to the feed barn. There the closed door prevented the flames from coming into the stable. They spotted my father half-conscious from the smoke. He had lost his direction. Just as the two reached him, the door of the feed barn burst open and huge flames came in. They rushed out, leading my father. The next day the stable was a horrifying sight. We children were not permitted to go look, and I am grateful for that. The investigation showed evidence of arson, but the arsonist was never discovered.

Another sad and unusual event counts among my childhood memories. Our dairy man owned a short-haired German pointer named Lord. This dog was his constant companion. He had trained the dog and had won first prize at a showing. The dog was outstanding. For example, his master could send Lord to the food shop in the village, one kilometer from the estate, with a basket, list and money. There he would be noticed at the entrance of the shop, and the shop owner would fill the basket with the desired items. Lord always brought everything correctly home, even meat and sausages. My father periodically sent to Germany for forest rangers, because they were trustworthy and skilled woodsmen. One of them, a young man and only child of a widow, arrived at Hummelshof several days before my story begins. His district and the house that belonged with it were located about sixteen kilometers deep in the forest on a lake that harbored many wild ducks. One day he wished to shoot a few ducks for himself and asked to borrow Lord, since he had no dog of his own. He promised to return the dog in three days. Lord did not want to follow the strange man, but the dairyman ordered him to go and not to leave him. Lord complied with lowered head, his tail between his legs.

The separation was difficult for our dairyman, and he waited impatiently for the dog to return. But on the third and fourth day the dog still had not returned. He was terribly worried. On the afternoon of the fifth day, two men came to see the estate manager, and they told him of a strange and terrible incident. They had been in the process of mowing grass in the forest when a dog appeared at the edge of the meadow, barked loudly, and ran back into the woods. After a small interval he appeared again, barked again and whined, and ran back into the woods. The two men decided to follow the dog, should he appear again. Soon the dog appeared in the same manner, and they followed him. When they reached the lake, they were met by a horrifying sight—a man lay shot at the edge of the lake.

When our estate manager reached the lake, the dog was still lying beside the corpse, and only when he told him "Go home," did Lord run back to the estate. The dairyman told us later that when the dog came to him at the estate he behaved as if crazed, howling, whining, jumping up on him, and rolling, whining, on the ground. The police searched without success for the murderer of the ranger. Ten years later a man came to see my father to inform him of something that for years had robbed him of peace and lay heavily on his soul. During the night, this man's father had died. He told my father that his father had shot the ranger ten years ago, and that his father had been a poacher, having poached hundreds of wild animals in our forest.

6. School at Home

Until now I have told about myself as a small child, when, aside from Mali, I was taken care of by the much loved Mlle. Vouta from Switzerland. But when I turned six years old, everything changed. Mlle. Vouta left us to return to her homeland, which was terribly painful to me. To take her place Mlle. Jeanne arrived from Paris, but we did not like her nearly as well. I now had to share a room with my two older sisters, Irene and Madeleine, and my mother gave me the strict order that I was to obey them. My sisters were delighted, but for me it was awful, because, as a result, I had to serve my sisters hand and foot. When I refused, they beat me or used other means to make me obey them. Children can indeed be very cruel without realizing it.

One day in September my parents came to us with an elderly gentleman. He was introduced to us as our tutor, Herr Herbig. He had previously taught for many years at the *Gymnasium* (high school) in Fellin, where my father had been a student. He later told us that our father had been one of his favorite students. Herr Herbig looked at us very seriously and skeptically and said, "I have always taught only boys and know nothing about girls, but I will treat you like boys and you will learn to jump over chairs and tables." He soon began his educational program which included daily gymnastics after the lessons. Aside from calisthenics, we did jumping, running, and exercises at the bar. I loved this activity and always looked forward to it.

Herr Herbig awoke us every morning out of deep slumber at fifteen minutes before seven. Still half-asleep, we got dressed, and the nanny combed our hair and braided it. From there we rushed to the dining room. Already seated at the table were Herr Herbig, Mlle. Jeanne, and the very nice Russian teacher, Vladimir Nicolaievitch. At precisely eight o'clock we had to be in the estate schoolroom, not one minute earlier or later. I learned to always be punctual to the minute. Herr Herbig received us with a stern expression. Sometimes all went well, but other times our ears were boxed until our heads hummed. The lessons were arranged according to the system of the *Gymnasium*, and at the end of each semester we had to take exams.

Lunch was served at exactly 12:30. We children had to assemble downstairs, washed and combed. Punctually the old butler opened the large French doors to the dining room and, in a very dignified manner, informed my mother that lunch was served. Each of us went into the dining room and stood behind our chair, waiting for Mother. Only when she was seated were the children allowed to sit down, but without the least bit of noise. We were strictly forbidden to speak during the meal. The courses were served by the butler and the footman, Ferdi, while my parents conversed with the guests almost always present at our table. After my mother declared the meal ended, the children had to thank her with a curtsy and a hand kiss.

Part of our daily school life was an afternoon promenade from around one to four o'clock, accompanied by Herr Herbig. He was a great lover of nature and a learned botanist and biologist. He taught us the names and habits of the birds and other animals, as well as of the trees, plants and flowers. Once we had returned to the house, we were served milk and bread and then we had to return to the schoolroom. There we had to do our homework under the supervision of our teacher. After we had finished our work, he often read to us until dinner time. I remember especially the interesting and exciting stories of the American Indians from James Fenimore Cooper's "Leather Stocking." At seven o'clock dinner was served. After dinner, we all assembled in the living room and gathered around the table. There we alternately read a story out loud while the others busied themselves with handicrafts.

Six weeks before exams, I began to study and review the material learned—we had to learn much by rote. In my fear of failing the exams, I would get up at five in the morning. In the spring I loved to climb the many stairs to the tower where, with much effort, I opened the heavy dormer which led to an open platform. There I was greeted by a heavenly view of the forest and blue mountain ridges. The sun had risen and the dew on the grass and leaves glittered like thousands of diamonds. The air was filled with the songs of birds. My school work was waiting, so I could never contemplate this magnificent view for very long. I would sit down on the floor, hold my ears closed and thus I studied and studied. At a quarter to seven I had to be back in our bedroom, for Herr H. must not know of my escapades. In class, of course, I could hardly keep my eyes open, but I had the satisfaction of doing well in all my exams. Besides that, I learned to concentrate, which was of great help throughout my life.

Classes and school work left us little time to play, and we always greeted the three months of summer vacation with joy. Then we were again permitted to ride our ponies, which were forbidden during the school term. But in the summer we had complete freedom, as long as we appeared punctually, clean and combed, for meals.

I was a very lonely child and longed endlessly for playmates. My older sisters found me bothersome and always chased me away. My two younger sisters and my brother were four, six, and eight years younger than I, and of no interest to me as playmates. In my need for companionship, I turned to our horses. I visited them every day and was always greeted with a gentle, cheerful whinnying, for they knew I had black bread for them and I patted their shiny necks. I kissed and hugged my favorite horse, Hopsassa, which she quietly tolerated.

My second set of friends were the dogs, who always greeted me with joy and often accompanied me on my walks. One of my daily walks led to the orchard filled with many fruit trees and berry bushes. Also, the forest was like a great friend to me; I wandered in it endlessly, on foot or on horseback. The forest quietly consoled me for everything that I missed in my life, for all that made me sad and despairing, and for the overwhelming loneliness that I experienced day in and day out. The trees swaying in the wind, the deep peace that surrounded me, and especially the spiritual strength emanating from the nature around me—what the Indians call the "Great Spirit" and which has many other names—all this had a healing and calming effect on me and filled my heart with joy, and sometimes bliss.

But the forest became more and more a necessity to me. I was intensely shy with people and I had no trust in them. I only had contact with superiors, who were cold and indifferent towards me and my sisters. The ladies who visited my mother had to be greeted by us with a curtsy and a hand kiss, and the men with a curtsy. After the greeting we had to leave the room silently, or politely answer questions. All this led me in a dangerous direction. I became more and more a creature of the wilderness. I hopelessly yearned for playmates, and yet I was always alone.

My mother appeared to me to be cold and proud. She lacked the motherly and loving warmth that every child needs and which I deeply missed. When she called me from my play with her hard, cold voice, I immediately ran to her as fast as I could, terribly frightened. Usually some admonishments or punishments awaited me. My mother once said to all of us children, "You need not love me, but you must fear me."

7. Christmas

In spite of everything, there were also light, happy and gay periods in our childhood, times which all of us remember with joy. One of these memorable times was the yearly celebration of Christmas at Hummelshof. My mother had an extraordinary ability to celebrate the great holidays of Christmas and Easter. Before Christmas, we were allowed to help shape the spice cookies, which were baked in great masses because we also celebrated Christmas with our workers and their families on the 23rd of December. This took place in the large dining room, with a decorated Christmas tree, presents and many sweets.

But the day we impatiently awaited was the 24th of December, when we would receive presents and sweets. Only on Christmas Eve and on our birthdays did we ever receive sweets. The day before Christmas, the gardener Ronk brought an enormous tree from the forest and placed it at the end of the ballroom in front of the huge, wide mirrors that reached to the ceiling. Every year was exactly the same; it had to be just like the previous Christmas or else it would not have been a real Christmas for us.

In the morning we decorated the tree. The gardener and Ferdi helped with long ladders, beginning the decorating at the top. We children managed the lower sections. We felt as if we had been transported into a magical land, and we could hardly wait for the evening. When the decorating was finished, two hundred white candles were placed on the tree—they would burn for four hours—and finally the thin, silver tinsel that looked like glittering silver breath was hung. These activities occupied the whole morning.

When it was finished, we had to leave the room, and the gigantic double doors were closed behind us. Now my mother occupied herself with the rest of the preparations. For each of us children a table was placed under the tree, covered with a white tablecloth, and on it were placed our presents. In the meantime we had to take a long walk after lunch with our teacher into the deeply snowed-over *Mühlenwald* ("forest of the mill") as part of the tradition. In the forest reigned deep silence. The snow muffled all sounds, but it crunched under our boots. No animal was to be seen. Now and then we noticed the trail of a rabbit or some other animal.

When we returned home, we cleaned ourselves and dressed up and then we were served hot chocolate and Christmas "Stollen"—a traditional sweet bread made with lots of butter, eggs, sugar, almonds and saffron. During all this time, our expectations reached a feverish peak and the moment would finally arrive when my mother announced the lighting of the candles. We lined up in the hall and could see through the two salons that led to the ballroom, which was around the corner. It became lighter and lighter as the candles were being lit, and we became more and more excited as the lovely smell of the fir tree drifted toward us. Then suddenly we heard my mother play on the piano the beautiful Christmas song "Silent Night," which was the signal that we were allowed to enter the room.

We moved as if in a dream. The room lay before us with sparkling lights. A second tree glittered, and winked at us out of the mirror. We then had to gather around my mother and sing two carols. After that we were permitted to look at our presents, and we would notice with delight that all our wishes had been fulfilled. Unfortunately, Christmas Eve would soon be over, and everything would be back to normal.

8. A Change Takes Place

Something happened when I was ten or eleven years old that would prove to be a change for the better in my life. Our tutor, Herr Herbig, could no longer continue teaching because of his age. For this reason he left us and returned to his home town of Koblenz in Germany. He was replaced by Fräulein Jung, an intelligent, educated person equipped with teaching certificate and experience. She was my mother's age and very fat. I was very shy at the time, plagued by terrible inferiority complexes.

Fräulein Jung addressed me as Miss Ellen, which seemed strange to me, and she treated me as an equal. Until then I had been used to being nothing, someone who was not permitted to participate in conversation. With Fräulein Jung I was even permitted to ask questions—although I hardly dared—questions which had long burned inside of me. She said to me one day, perhaps to give me courage, "Ask me as many questions as you please. You have not yet asked me a stupid question." Yet it was some time before I trusted her, but she had a way with children like me. I still remember the happy hours I was allowed to spend with her in her room. Without timidity, I could speak with her about everything. We even had discussions on philosophical questions.

Mlle. Jeanne was still a part of our household. She had succeeded in winning the confidence of our mother, yet she frequently created very uncomfortable times for us through her intrigues. Our Russian teacher, Vladimir Nicolaievitch, was a cheerful and kind person. He never made life difficult for us. We often gathered in the park, and he would play on his balalaika a *kazachok* (Russian national dance). He danced and sang, while we children danced wildly around him.

We had a very good coachman by the name of Peter Ilvis. He loved the horses and took excellent care of them. He was around twenty-five years old at the time of this story. His best friend of the same age, who was called Sokka August after the farm of his father, was also a horse lover. He owned a beautiful stallion which he used, especially on Sundays, for church-going. These stallions were called *kiriko-tek*, Estonian for "church stallions." The two young men were in constant competition as far as the horses went.

It was the end of March and everything was covered by deep snow, although a thaw had begun as the sun was getting warmer. The roadways were very bad with slush and potholes. Once a week Peter drove me one and one-half hours to the small town named Walk for piano lessons. This time he had taken me by sleigh, pulled by a thoroughbred. On our return trip we must have hit a deep pothole, because the sleigh turned over and we flew in our double layer of furs into the deep, wet snow. At this moment Peter's archrival Sokka August drove by in his sleigh, pulled by that beautiful "church" stallion. He looked smilingly at us and vanished into the distance. Peter lifted himself out of the snow and in despair called out, "My God! My God! Sokka August has seen this!" Never mind that I was hopelessly stuck in the wet snow with my double layer of furs handicapping my every move.

During the summer our riding and carriage horses were ridden to the river by Peter Ilvis and his stable boys. We children also rode along bareback and galloped to the river accompanied by Peter's small mutt, Flock. He was an ugly little fellow, but energetic and happy. At the river the horses were led into the water, washed, scrubbed and allowed to swim. When this was done and the horses were back on land, Flock's great moment came. He ran to the coachman and jumped and begged. Peter wanted to be left alone, but the dog would not listen. So he said "all right," grabbed the little mutt by his neck and twirled him several times around, and threw him high in the air and into the river. Flock swam to land and begged again and again for the same thrill.

I loved to read, especially Grimm's fairy tales and heroic myths, but also the animal tales of Ernest Thompson Seton. I had the habit of going far into the woods with my book, always followed by the dogs. I would sit on the river bank and lose myself in a world of fairy tales and heroes. Thus passed several years, and then came a great change in our lives.

9. The Year 1905

In 1905 the Russo-Japanese war ended in the defeat of Russia and was followed by a bloody revolution. In the Baltics as well there was fighting, and many estates were burned and the owners were murdered.

My mother decided to take refuge in Germany with the children, while my father remained on the estate with the brothers of my mother. However, we were all relieved to find out later that life continued normally at Hummelshof and nothing bad happened there. In Germany we lived in the ancient, fortress-like castle of my uncle Baron von Gaisberg, who was Lord Chamberlain to the king of Württemberg, William II (1848-1921), and was married to my mother's sister. They had two beautiful daughters, Antonie and Louise, and two younger sons, Otto and Eric, both later killed in World War I. The family's permanent residence was in Cannstatt, a suburb of Stuttgart, where the King's residence was as well. They spent only a few summer weeks at the castle. King William abdicated in late 1918 and Württemberg soon after joined the Weimar Republic.

My mother remained one year in Germany, during which time the Tsar's troops, the Cossacks, had restored order and peace in the

Baltics. To my horror and despair, when my mother returned to Hummelshof in 1906, she left Madeleine and me behind with our relatives. Madeleine, who was already eighteen, left shortly thereafter for finishing school in Switzerland and a year later transferred to one in England. For two years I was to attend school in Cannstatt, but it turned out to be disastrous for me. Since I had never been in a regular school, to be in a class full of strange children who stared at me totally bewildered and estranged me. In addition, I had trouble understanding the south German dialect of the children and the teacher. I was in despair and terribly homesick.

My relatives with whom I lived were very nice to me and tried to help me adjust. In their home I once had a very strange experience which made a deep impression on me: one day, as I wandered through various empty salons which led to my uncle's writing room, I suddenly saw a large pool of blood on the floor of one of the rooms, and there was blood dripping from the ceiling. Horrified, I ran to tell my aunt, who rushed to the second story of the building where an old general lived with his family. There she learned that the general had shot himself.

One day my old tutor, Herr Herbig, came to visit me from Koblenz. We took a walk together, and he must have noticed my desperately unhappy state of mind. I can only assume that he informed my parents, for soon after they arranged for me to return home. It had been two years since I had left Hummelshof. I was incredibly happy to return. Nothing seemed to have changed—the horses, the dogs, and especially my wonderful forest—all was there as I had left it. Fräulein

Jung was still instructing my younger sisters and brother, and I resumed visiting her in her room where I could talk and talk and philosophize.

10. School in Riga

When I was fifteen years old and had two more years of schooling ahead of me, I was sent to Riga in what is now Latvia. There I was enrolled in a well-known boarding school for girls, run by two elderly sisters, Hilda and Marie. They were friendly ladies who gave me much warmth and trust. In my new school, I first shared a room with two other girls, both older, and best of friends. One was my cousin, a beautiful girl, and the other was big, strong-boned and rough. She loved to tyrannize other girls and often attacked them physically. I was one of those unfortunate victims.

These two girls had the habit of talking late into the night, not letting me sleep. All my complaints did not help. One night, when I was desperately tired and I had asked them once more to be quiet, big Irene came with a jug of water and poured it all over me and my bed. The water actually created puddles in my bed. Eventually, I was given different quarters with peaceful girls, and there I stayed until the end of my school years.

My longing for the country, especially Hummelshof, never ceased. I could not get used to being in a city—surrounded by dead stones instead of living earth and nature. Yet I accepted the fact that I had to finish school and stay in Riga. I never protested that, except once. It happened after our Easter vacation was over, and I had to leave Hummelshof during my favorite season. My father brought me to the train station where he asked an acquaintance, taking the same train, to keep an eye on me. Once in the train, I noticed my school friend Lio in the company of a student whom I also knew. They were sitting in a nearby compartment, and I got permission from my companion to sit with my friends.

As the train sped further and further away from my beloved home, my heart sank. The thought of returning to the dusty, crowded city filled me with desperation. As we approached Wenden, Lio told us that she had an aunt and uncle who lived near that charming little town. Her uncle was head forester and had his home in the forest of Wenden. This suddenly gave me a crazy idea. I said to my friends how great it would be to leave the train at Wenden and to visit Lio's relatives. At first they did not want to hear about it, but in the end we were all excited and decided to go ahead with the plan. I said nothing to the lady in charge of me. Instead, we sneaked out of the train in Wenden, and Lio telephoned her uncle. It was already getting dark. Lio's uncle said we were welcome to visit him, and so we rented a carriage and started on the long drive through endless forests that seemed to go as far as we could see in the dark. When we finally arrived, we had a warm welcome. We were very excited, but confessed our escapade to Lio's uncle. He suggested that he telephone our school so that the two sisters would not worry, and he would arrange for us to arrive two days later. This done, we were able to enjoy our last days of freedom.

The next day Lio's uncle accompanied us as we took a long walk through the woods and along the river. We spent a second night with our wonderful hosts, and then we had to leave. As we got into the train, I noticed with horror my uncle Paul von Stryk, my mother's brother, who had been at Hummelshof when I left. When he saw me he exclaimed, "Where are you coming from? Why aren't you in Riga?" I said that I would explain everything but first I had to find a seat, and so I joined my friends in an empty compartment. The train had hardly started when my uncle called me out into the hallway and demanded an explanation. I told him of our adventure. He looked terribly serious and I expected the worst. But suddenly he laughed and asked me if I would like to go to the circus in Riga with him and a friend that same evening. Of course I wanted to very much. I promised to meet my uncle at his hotel.

Once back in the compartment, I started to get quite worried and nervous as the train approached Riga. I was sure they would throw me out of the boarding school, and that I would be too late for the circus. On top of it all I was terribly bored with Lio's friend who sat across from me. I started to argue with her about, of all things, how to bring up children.

When we arrived at the boarding school, we immediately were sent for by Miss Marie. She began with a long speech admonishing us and suggesting that it probably was all my idea. Of course I could not deny that. During her speech I became more and more nervous and fidgety because it started to get late. Finally, I could no longer contain myself and asked, "Miss Marie, may I go to the circus tonight with my uncle?" She looked at me speechless, but then she laughed and said, "All right, go! You are really hopeless." Thanking her, I rushed out of her office, arranged my hair a little, and ran to my uncle's hotel. He and his friend were just on the point of leaving. I told him that all had gone well at the school. He took my arm with a friendly grin, and the three of us went off to the circus. When my mother came to Riga and found out about my adventure, I had to live through a few uncomfortable moments; but soon it was all forgotten.

11. Return to Hummelshof

When my schooling in Riga was finished, I returned to Hummelshof. I was given my own room, which I divided into a sleeping and living area. There I felt at home and comfortable. From the large windows I had a view directly on the park, composed mostly of linden trees with many high branches where songbirds made their nests. In the spring the songs of thousands of birds frequently woke me very early in the morning. I would get up and lean out of the open window. A fog would rise from the park, and I could hear the rumbling mating calls of the heath cock. The air was filled with the intoxicating perfume of the earth, the trees and the flowering bushes.

My parents entrusted me with the care of the sick among our employees, for our family physician lived far away and was overworked. He was only able to come for very serious illnesses. I frequently asked him for advice by telephone. Otherwise, I had a cabinet full of medications and a medical lexicon. Thus equipped, I did the best I could. I was delighted to find that our employees soon developed a trust in me, and I was frequently called on to take care of various medical problems.

I also established a little school for children, where I gave instructions for three hours every morning. The children had come with their parents from the south of Russia and spoke German, which made it hard for them to adjust to the Estonian schools. Dating from the time of Catherine the Great, there had been a sizeable colony of German immigrants in Ukraine. In addition, I cared for these children in other ways. I took them for walks in the woods, or we cooked lunch together on a small stove in the park. This would usually consist of a vegetable soup. The children and I would gather vegetables from the garden, clean them, and cut them up. The meal would end with a dessert. Thus the children and I would spend wonderful hours in the park and delighted in the lunch prepared by ourselves.

My sister Madeleine, while at her English finishing school, made the acquaintance of a young man from an old and distinguished English family, Ralph Montagu-Scott. She soon was engaged to him and an elaborate wedding took place at Hummelshof in 1908. My oldest sister, Irene, became engaged to Theodor Baron von der Osten-Sacken, and they were married soon after Madeleine. Irene and her husband moved to

Riga and had two daughters, Nanuschka and Ljuba. Madeleine and her husband lived in London and later had two sons, Michael and Dunstan.

During this time at home, my mother did not change her attitude toward me. She continued to make me feel that I was worthless, and I was not to speak. I was filled with bitterness, and I was lonely and helpless. I had such a desire for love and recognition, especially from my mother; yet she only approached me with coldness and strictness. It pains me that, as I am writing this, I cannot judge my mother in a better light. There is no doubt that the lack of love from my mother had an unfortunate effect on my whole life. But now all this is forgotten and I think of my mother with much love. In her own way she loved us all, but it was not in her nature to show it. However, I have much to thank her for, especially that she taught me self-discipline and self-control. Unfortunately, the methods of child rearing of the period among the upper classes were very misguided. Much damage was done to the children's personalities and self-esteem. One must say that today the opposite is taking place, also with unfortunate results. It is best to find a middle ground. Children need strictness, discipline and justice, but no less do they need love and recognition. Over-indulging children is a terrible disservice to them. Life is hard and without consideration. How can a child, to whom nothing has been refused, then face life with all its difficulties and disappointments?

I was very fond of my father. I was always delighted when he spent some time at home, which was infrequently. My parents had very different characters. My father was always cheerful and outgoing. He had a wonderful sense of humor and knew how to make friends with everyone. The upbringing of the children he left entirely to my mother, however, and he supported her in everything. As a result, I did not at first develop a close relationship with my father and kept my distance from him.

He had the habit of rising at 5:30 in the morning to work at his desk and take care of all his paperwork. Sometimes I heard him humming a song as he descended the staircase. Soon after, Ferdi would come to start a fire in the fireplace, to bring the steaming samovar, and to set the breakfast table. My father was a great drinker of tea. He always prepared it himself with tea that he ordered directly from China. The tea would arrive beautifully wrapped in variously colored silk bags with gold- colored Chinese writing on them. We children always looked at the bags with utter delight and respect. Then my father would tell us jokingly that this tea had been transported on camel back from China to Russia.

12. Mountain Cock Hunt

Among the annual events on our estate was one that left a great impression on me: the hunt of the mountain cock during mating season in April. Occasionally, my father would take me along. When it was still dark and the sky was covered with sparkling stars, we would start out in a carriage pulled by my father's hunting horse, Emir. Our path took us deep into the forest. Once we arrived, the horse was covered with a blanket and tied up, and on foot we would noiselessly approach the mating areas. It was still the middle of the night—the silence would rush in our ears. Now and then it was broken by the strange, ghostly tone made by the back and forth flight of the night swallows. Soon we could hear the mating calls. We would advance with utmost care.

The mountain cock is a very curious bird. While making the mating call, it hears and sees nothing, and we would have time to take three steps. Then it makes a ticking sound, at which time it listens for sounds with its very sharp hearing. Being a very shy animal, if the hunters are not totally silent and motionless, it will disappear instantly. As we approached closer and closer, we could see the cock high in a tree, a black silhouette against the sky that was beginning to lighten. The feathers of its tail were spread out like a fan. Then there would be the sound of a shot, and the bird would come crashing down, hitting the ground with a dull thud. At this moment I always felt sad, and would have liked to see the bird continue living. It is a beautiful bird, about ten to twelve pounds, with glittering black, green, and blue feathers, and thick red eyebrows.

The mountain cock bagged, we would return to the carriage. Now it would be light and the whole forest would resound with the song of birds. We rode back to the house against the rising sun.

13. A Wish Comes True

One day when I was around seventeen, we received the news that Herr Herbig, our old teacher, had died, and that he had left a sum of money for each of my sisters and me. For years we had had no news from him, and did not know how he spent his last years in Germany or what was the cause of his death. The inheritance from Herr Herbig enabled me to realize a wish that I had had for a long time: I wanted to have my own riding horse. A well-known horse expert, therefore, purchased for me a five-year-old thoroughbred Arab mare named Suleika. She was as beautiful as a picture, of gold-red coloring, with a white stripe from the forehead down to the nostrils, white socks on her hind legs, and a beautiful, slender tail, typical of thoroughbreds. She still had to be broken in, but since I had taken riding lessons in Wiesbaden and Riga, I was able to start right away. Every day I rode her for one hour in the "ménage." At the beginning she reacted strongly and impatiently to my attempts, but she taught me something very important: to be patient, no matter how she behaved. Thus we slowly made progress. I was not satisfied until Suleika was able to go from a halt into a slow gallop with her weight on her hind legs, and then from the slow gallop to a sudden halt. In addition, I taught her to gallop at the same tempo around my sleeping dog. She managed this wonderfully, and I practiced this later in the forest, riding around a tree.

One day I decided to ride Suleika deep into the woods, accompanied by my English setter, Bingo. We were trotting on a path along a canal filled with water and beyond it was a swamp. If one fell into this swamp one could vanish forever. One could walk the swamp only if he knew how to do it, that is, by walking from grass hill to grass hill between the silky, fresh, green terrain, which, for all its beauty, was fatal to anyone who stepped on it, because it pulled everything and everybody deep into its bowels like quicksand. Suddenly, Suleika shied and wildly tried to jump across the canal and into the swamp. It might mean certain death if she succeeded. I fought her impulse desperately, getting weaker from trying to hold her back. I turned to see what had frightened her, and there, about ten meters away, was a glorious moose with tremendous antlers pointed toward my barking dog. I was in a no-win situation: fighting with my horse while at the same time trying to take in as long as possible this beautiful picture of moose and dog. Then suddenly the moose majestically and slowly turned around and trotted off. Suleika calmed down and all was well again.

14. Woiseck

In 1912 an event took place in my life that was to give it a totally new direction. My cousin Toni von Gaisberg, who was visiting from Germany, and I traveled in the company of my aunt Ida to the city of Fellin to see the horse races. The races were followed by a sumptuous dinner and ball. At the dinner, I happened to sit next to an elderly gentleman, Leo von zur Mühlen, who engaged me in a lively conversation. At the end he asked me whether I would like to visit his estate, Woiseck. He said that I could travel there after the ball with him and his two daughters, whom I had not yet met. I could not come right out and say that I did not feel like visiting his estate at all, that I was anxious to return to Hummelshof, to my beloved forest and unspoiled nature. I thanked him politely, and tried to explain that my parents were expecting me home, and it would be impossible for me to come with him. He paid no attention to my excuses. Instead, he accompanied me to the telephone, and I had to call and ask permission of my parents. My parents granted permission, and thus my fate was sealed.

It was three o'clock in the morning when the carriage appeared, pulled by four fiery young stallions. The gentleman's daughters, Illa and Nello, more or less the same age as I, took the front seats, paid no attention to me, and slept the whole trip. I sat next to the father, filled with dark thoughts, hoping that the restless horses which were difficult to hold would swerve the carriage so that I would be thrown out and killed. But nothing happened. It was a glorious September morning; the sun's rays glittered on the dew-covered spider webs. At about eight o'clock in the morning we arrived at Woiseck. The lovely old and very large mansion impressed me as friendly and comfortable. It was surrounded by carefully tended gardens and majestic old trees.

At the entrance to the house was a glass veranda where we were greeted by the lady of the house. She suffered from an incurable disease that softened the bones, and she could only move about on crutches. The breakfast table was set with hot coffee waiting for us. I felt much better after we had our coffee and breakfast. Illa and Nello took me between them and showed me the house and their two rooms with lovely furniture, one a bedroom and the other a sitting room. I was to share these with them.

The house was divided into two wings by a very large hall. In the right wing lived the wife of the gentleman. She had many rooms there, including a large, rococo-style ballroom. In the left wing lived the husband with his mistress. There, as well, were many rooms including the dining room and a smaller salon. At meal times the master of the house appeared with his mistress, while his wife usually had her meals in her rooms. To me this situation was very strange and astounding, especially when my host belittled his wife in the presence of guests. It was such a contrast to the never-failing politeness and love that my father showed towards my mother. Eventually, I realized that my host was an outright tyrant, not only towards his family, but also towards the servants and employees.

There were five sons in the family in addition to the daughters, Illa and Nello. Two were married and lived on their own estates; one was an engineer in Riga, one a businessman in St. Petersburg, and one was pursuing his studies in Munich. The two daughters were the youngest of all the siblings. The wife was a very intelligent woman, full of humor, and very religious. She had accepted her fate with astounding strength. Never did I hear her complain.

I soon became good friends with the two girls. It was the first true friendship in my life. In my shyness, it was hard for me to believe at first that they enjoyed being in my company. Yet they refused to let me leave, and I remained with the family for three weeks instead of the planned three days. In spite of the fact that we lived far apart (a whole day's travel by carriage and rail), we remained excellent friends and saw each other frequently. They visited me at Hummelshof, and I often returned to Woiseck. In addition, they had at their disposal an apartment in the university town of Dorpat, in the house of their father's brother. I frequently stayed there with Illa and Nello during the "season" of balls and parties, that is, from the first of January to the beginning of Lent, and together we would attend the various social activities.

These times were always extremely exhausting. Almost every evening there was a ball and we would dance until morning. During the day, as well, there were many activities, such as riding in "troika" on the frozen river. (A troika can be either a sleigh or carriage pulled by three horses, the middle horse being a fast trotter while the two outside horses are galloping.) Up to a point I tolerated the festivities. But our dance partners were very young students and they were of little interest to me. In the end, I would invent a plausible excuse and return to Hummelshof, refusing any further invitations. I had grown up alone, and solitude had become a necessity. The forest, the stillness, the purity of nature, all this attracted me like a magnet.

It was at one of these balls, however, that things turned out differently. I had just been contemplating returning to the country, when I noticed a group of girls that I knew. I joined the group, and there was a young man whom I had not met. He was playing the guitar and singing with a fascinating voice. I suddenly learned the meaning of the saying "love at first sight." The young man was named Nicko von Pilar, and we became good friends. He later told me that he also had loved me from the moment he had set eyes on me. We now had wonderful times together, for Illa and Nello also had special friends, Erich von Kursell and Rolf von Oettingen. But only Nello ended up marrying her Rolf. Nicko and I also had plans to marry, but fate and World War I tore us apart, and we each went our separate ways.

For some time now I had become interested in religion. I believed in all that I had learned as a child—God, Christ, and the angels. But this was no longer enough for me. I experienced the healing effect of the strong, spiritual strength emanating from nature, and I had many questions: What is the source of the energy that makes everything grow? Where does life come from and where does it lead? What happens to man after death?—and so on. I could not find satisfactory answers, and I had the feeling that spiritually I was living in a dark sack.

It was Illa and Nello who first introduced me to Anthroposophy and the writings of its founder, Austrian-born Dr. Rudolf Steiner. They had been told about Steiner by a neighbor, the wife of the local pastor, and she had given them his book *Theosophy*. I also began to read this work and, to my astonishment, all my questions were answered, and much more. I ordered other works by Rudolf Steiner and found them very difficult, dealing with the interrelationships between the spiritual and material world and the cosmos. I had to read his work twice, very carefully, before a light seemed to turn on inside me. This light became brighter and brighter the more I studied Anthroposophy, and it gave me strength and meaning to my later life.

15. The Sale of Hummelshof

One day in 1912, as I was driving through the woods with my father, he informed me that he had sold Hummelshof to a neighbor and friend, Count Frederick Berg, and had bought the estate, Peddeln, that bordered on the Hummelshof property. This news was a terrible blow to me, for losing Hummelshof meant losing everything that I loved and on which my whole life hung. Since we could continue living at Hummelshof for another two years, life continued as before. Yet the thought that soon we would lose it forever was almost intolerable to me. For my parents, managing this very large estate had become too much. They longed for a more quiet, less demanding way of life. Peddeln seemed to be ideal. It had a tremendous forest which earned cash for running the estate. The cattle and fields were oriented toward supporting the household, without exports, so that many fewer employees were needed.

My father had the small, old house on the estate torn down, and a larger, lovely house was built in the same location in the French chateau style. It was beautifully situated with a view of a lake-like dam, surrounded by forest. At the same time he had a large hothouse built, and an orchard was planted with hundreds of fruit trees. With the help of a landscape architect, plans were drawn up for a flowered terrace and other plantings around the house. I could understand my parents' desire to simplify their life, and our new home had a lot of charm. However, nothing could take the place of Hummelshof for me— it was my home!

I continued to see Illa and Nello frequently. In visiting Woiseck, I made the acquaintance of some of their brothers. The oldest, Victor, owned the neighboring estate of Eigstfer. In 1908 he was married to Hermine Countess Folliot de Crenneville-Poutet, who was a very unusual person. Her father was an Austrian diplomat, and she had therefore seen much of the world. The couple had no children, and the marriage was unhappy. After a few years, they were divorced. Victor later was happily married to a much younger person, Birutta Eichen, but they both perished near the end of World War II. Hermine went on to become a leftist writer, living for a while in her native Austria, but then having to flee eventually to England soon after the German annexation because of her anti-Nazi writings. She died there in 1951.

Another brother, Egolf, was a very handsome young man, unmarried, and charming with women. Now and then he visited Woiseck. Arved, the third brother, also came to visit. He owned the estate Sennen and was married to Elizabeth Countess von Keller, the daughter of a man who was later the commander of the Russian troops on the southern front in World War I. She was a beautiful and cultured woman. The couple had two sons and a daughter, but this marriage as well ended in divorce. The fourth brother, Moritz, lived in St. Petersburg. He was single and a business man. The youngest, Max, nicknamed

Macki, was to return soon to Woiseck after finishing his forestry studies in Munich.

16. The Outbreak of World War I

In June 1914 I received an invitation from Illa and Nello to visit Woiseck. Macki had returned home and would enjoy some company. I gladly accepted, for I was curious to meet the one member of this eccentric family whom I had not yet met, especially since I liked the others so well. When I arrived, I met a very handsome, charming young man. We got along quite well, and every day we took long rides on some of the thoroughbred horses of the estate, or we passed hours sitting with the two sisters in conversation. I remained there for a week, and then returned to Hummelshof.

Then one day our wonderful, peaceful life was suddenly shattered with the terrible news of the assassination in Serbia of the Austrian Crown Prince, followed by declarations of war among the major powers. It seemed as if overnight all of Europe was in turmoil. A wave of restlessness and distress spread throughout Russia, and young men were being drafted. Macki and his brother Mori joined the Guardian Dragoons, a Life Guard regiment of the Tsarina. For a while they were stationed at the Alexander Palace in Tsarskoe Selo, the royal family's palace complex outside St. Petersburg, but later the regiment was sent to the front, where it remained for much of the war.

The Tsarina and the grand duchesses of her court all established their own hospitals, where they treated and cared for the wounded. Many estates followed their example, including Hummelshof, by banding together to establish and financially support small clinics in different areas. I volunteered my services, and simultaneously took a nursing course with a physician. At the makeshift clinic there was a trained nurse, and Fräulein Jung was the bookkeeper. The area physician came twice a week. Since we did not have a permanent physician on the premises, only lightly wounded soldiers were sent to us, and we had little problem taking care of them.

The wounded arrived on the estate directly from the front. They were unbelievably dirty, covered with lice and dirty bandages. They were put immediately into the sauna where the army surgeon cut their hair and beards, scrubbed them, and then they were given clean pajamas and robes. Only then were they permitted into the clinic. With the help of the physician we treated the wounds, and then they were given a meal and rest.

These soldiers originated from all parts of Russia—it was a colorful mix of peoples. There were the tall, blond and blue-eyed White Russians from the north; the smaller, dark-haired ones from Ukraine; the Cossacks from the Don River and Siberia; the Tatars from the Crimea; oriental types from the Caucasus; Siberian Mongols with slanted eyes and broad cheek bones; Kirghiz nomads; and Estonians and Latvians. Many of these soldiers were quite primitive, were unable to read or write, and their manners left a lot to be desired. To counteract their rudeness we were especially polite, and this worked wonders. After a while they also behaved politely toward us.

The Russian people are very musical and on any occasion they will sing. No wonder, then, that even in our little clinic the good singing voices found each other very quickly, and a small chorus came into being, singing the wonderful Russian folk songs. Every room in the clinic had an icon hanging on the wall. On Saturday evenings a little oil lamp was lit under the icon, and in this soft light the chorus would sing in subdued tones. I always longed to just sit down and listen, but work had to be done. One of the enjoyable routines of my day was the daily visits, together with Fräulein Jung, to see the patients. We talked with them and got to know them, and they enjoyed our visits very much. After one year, however, all the private clinics were shut down. The reason given was that the soldiers were spoiled there and became useless for war.

17. Farewell to Hummelshof

The moment had arrived and my parents were preparing for their move to Peddeln. Everywhere one turned there were boxes and furniture, and the day of the move approached rapidly. Some of our horses, including my beautiful Suleika, had been requisitioned by the military. It was as if everything was falling apart like a fragile house of cards.

On the day of our departure, the forty peasants who had leased land from my father arrived in the morning and presented him with a leather-bound address of gratitude, signed by all of them. Frequently my father had not demanded the rent for the land when there was a bad harvest, and he had helped in many other ways as well. These forty peasants had come with their horses and carts and helped with our move to Peddeln. It was a curious sight when we started on our way. At the start of the caravan was my parents' carriage where we children also rode, and this was followed by a long train of peasant carts and horses. Thus we advanced at a walking pace the twenty kilometers to Peddeln. (In today's geography, Hummelshof is located in Estonia and Peddeln just across the border in Latvia. Both estates are on local area maps under different but similar names.) When we arrived, all our furniture and belongings were stored because the house was not finished. While we waited for its completion, we lived in the renovated caretaker's house.

In the meantime, the German troops were winning on the eastern front, and the Russian troops were pulling back. As a consequence, there was a growing mistrust in the Baltics of German-speaking people such as ourselves. Many innocent people were arrested, accused of espionage and sent to Siberia by the Tsar's secret police. My parents, therefore, decided not to remain on the estate, but to move to Riga. They rented a big apartment, and we all moved there—my parents, my two younger sisters, my brother and myself. To our delight, Vladimir Nicolaievitch, our Russian teacher, also came with us. He was wonderful in keeping up our good spirits, playing his balalaika and singing and dancing. He was usually successful in cheering us up, but the life in the city was depressing to us. We took long walks, hoping to find areas resembling the countryside, but without success, because the city of Riga was very large.

My sisters attended school in Riga, while I started as an apprentice nurse at the large Red Cross Hospital. By this time the German troops were only a few kilometers from Riga, and there was bitter fighting outside the city. Wounded soldiers dragged themselves into the city and lay in the streets by the thousands, waiting to be brought to the hospital. The hospital was quickly overflowing with patients, taxing the energy of the physicians and nurses to the extreme. There was very little time to train me, and I had to help out where I could. I frequently came to the point of fainting when the old bandages of the seriously wounded soldiers were changed, and an overwhelming stench filled the overheated rooms. There were wounded who screamed day and night, and only stopped as they received chloroform when their bandages were changed. I was filled with pity for these poor suffering men; I could almost feel their pain. A young surgeon there warned me not to let myself feel pity. He told me, "All of us who work in the hospital must have an indifferent attitude, otherwise we will not be able to tolerate this." I knew he was right, but I was unable to follow his advice. I was too unprepared for the gruesome, terrifying scenes I witnessed. During operations I had to assist in handing the surgeons the needed instruments. I had had no training. Usually there were four operations going on in the same room, and new wounded were brought in constantly. The fighting continued relentlessly and was so close to the city now that, in the evening, we could see the bright flashing from the artillery and the flares.

In the hospital, however, there was no time to pay attention to that. I worked this way for several months. But then I had such a terrible experience that I could not continue. German bombers appeared over the city on every clear, cloudless day, and dropped bombs. One time the bombs landed in a refugee camp and did terrible damage. I will describe several cases that I myself witnessed. We were in a large room with patients, taking care of some daily routines, when the doors opened and the ambulance personnel carried in terribly wounded people. The carriers' white uniforms were red with blood. There was a young woman dying, and her husband kept bending over her with the expression of a madman. When she had died, I brought him a glass of water to calm him, which he drank and then fled from the room. Another young woman, her head totally bashed in, gave birth to a stillborn child while she herself was dying. An old woman was brought in and placed in a chair. She collapsed and would have fallen, but another nurse and I supported her. We then noticed that her leg was in shreds. The physician examining her wanted to amputate immediately, but she would not give her consent. Only three days later, when blood poisoning had set in, did she consent. I helped during the operation. The whole leg was removed, but the woman died on the operating table.

With all this I could not continue. It was a horrifying episode in my life, and I never took up nursing again. Somewhat unwillingly, my parents gave me permission to go to Peddeln to recuperate from the ordeals I had gone through. Our old forester lived in the upper story of the house, and several other employees whom I had known since my childhood were there, so I would not be alone. When I arrived it was winter. I was overcome with an incredible feeling of liberation. Profound peace reigned there, and the war seemed very far removed. I spent many hours skiing through the forest in the deep snow, accompanied by the dogs. I also did skijoring, which is to let oneself be pulled by a horse while standing on skis. The horse would go in full gallop, and the speed would create an indescribable joy within me. It had the same effect on the horse and the dogs, as we raced thus through the woods. I also spent much time reading.

This wonderful peace was interrupted one day, however. Nearby on the highway, an endless train of retreating military personnel was passing by day after day. One evening at around nine o'clock, our old forester came to me very excited and asked me to close all the windows and pull the curtains, to lock the door of my room and to remain there. Some of the retreating Russian troops were approaching the house. These troops, beaten by the enemy, could be very dangerous, especially if any half-wild Siberian Mongols were among them. It was a bitterly cold night, and deep snow covered the earth. Soon our courtyard was filled with soldiers, horses and carts. On every tree horses were tethered. Around twelve thousand soldiers had settled in the surrounding fields and on the street. Everywhere one could see bonfires. Our house was entered by close to sixty officers, who were seeking warmth, food and hot tea to drink. I remained in my room with the door locked. When I awoke during the night, I heard steps in front of my door, going back and forth at an even pace. I was told the next morning that the commanding general had ordered a soldier to guard my door. The troops only remained the night and pulled out the following morning.

Soon after this incident, our old forester had to leave the estate for a short time. I remained alone in the house except for the house servants. One freezing morning, a troika turned from the street into our courtyard and stopped in front of the house. Out of the sled stepped a colonel, a younger officer, a civilian and our local policeman. They were followed by seven heavily armed *strashniki* (mounted police). These stationed themselves by the door of the living room where I was sitting. They were each holding rifles with bayonets fixed. The colonel said to me that I had been accused of espionage; did I admit my guilt? Of course, I denied the allegation. They then went outside in order to search the premises. Everything was turned upside down—the granary, the stables, and so on. In the kitchen the help were terribly afraid and excited, for they were all convinced I would be sent to Siberia. I tried to calm them, and assured them that I was completely innocent. I asked the cook to bake some cakes and prepare tea, and to send it in when the officers returned.

Two hours later the group returned to the house. The colonel addressed me furiously, "You lied to us. We have found something." I was at a loss to imagine what they could have found. At this point the tea and cakes were brought in. The colonel ignored them, took out a big sheet of paper and started to write. The younger officer and the civilians drank and ate with good appetite. I decided to be friendly with the young officer, since he seemed to have a more open disposition. He was a very impetuous Cherkessk from the Caucasus. We had a lively conversation, and hardly half an hour had passed when he proposed marriage to me. I thought he had gone a little too far there, and I had to hold him back. But I had to be extremely cautious not to offend him, because it was a question of my life, after all. So I told him that I could not accept his offer of marriage because one of my principles was never to marry. The fat colonel stopped writing, and laughingly listened to our conversation. Then he also accepted tea and ate some cake. The young officer began to recite to me his own poems, which he did with much pathos. Meanwhile, the colonel smiled in amusement at this scene.

After a while the group left, and we parted almost friends. Before they left, I asked the colonel what they had found. He said they had found a motor in the attic that could be used to make contact with the Germans. This was of course nonsense. My father had sent for this machine from Germany before the war, in order to set up a generator on the estate, because at that time we had no electricity. The motor was still in its box in the attic. The war had delayed putting the generator into service. I never heard anything more about this, and assume that I was declared innocent.

Shortly before Christmas 1915 I received an invitation from Illa and Nello to spend the holidays at Woiseck. I accepted gladly, because things had become a bit hot for me at Peddeln. The whole family was expected at Woiseck, including Macki, who was now on the front. There I passed a wonderful, carefree time. Woiseck was far removed from the front, and we noticed nothing of war there. After Christmas Eve, more friends arrived on the estate, and every day was a festival. Big sled parties were organized. The main object of these was to tip the sled over so that everyone was spilled into the deep snow. In the evenings we danced far into the night. Time passed like lightning and before we knew it, everyone had to leave again. But this was also the time of the beginning of the season in Dorpat, and Illa, Nello and I traveled there to continue the festivities. Unfortunately, Nicko was not there; he was fighting on the Russian southern front. I missed him very much.

Illa and Nello were irreplaceable friends for me at this time. Without them I would not have been able to withstand my loneliness and despair. They were always at my side, giving me courage. It was tragic that both sisters were ill. Nello, after many operations already, had growths that created much suffering for her. Illa had had a tuberculosis infection in one of her kidneys, which had to be removed, and later her spine was also infected. To cure this disease she had already spent three years in a Swiss sanatorium. Luckily, the cure seemed to have worked well, and she appeared to be quite healthy at this time.

After the season in Dorpat was over, my parents gave their consent for me to return to Peddeln, but with the condition that I would be accompanied by an elderly lady who would be my chaperone. After some searching, such a person was found and together we traveled to Peddeln. Spring was approaching. The days became warmer, and the snow began to melt. My companion was a very nice, friendly person, but we had nothing in common and lived more side by side than together. As always, I spent much time in the woods communicating with nature. I watched with joy the return of every bird from its southern winter home and the honking sounds from the formations of wild geese in the sky.

One day in early 1916 another invitation came from Illa and Nello to visit Woiseck, this time over the Easter holidays. Macki was expected and several other friends had been invited. And, as always, it was a joyful time. In the evenings we would stalk the woodcock from specially built stands in the forest, and early in the morning we undertook the hunt of the heathcock. Most every evening we also danced and danced.

At the time I did not know that these years were to be the loveliest, most carefree times of my life, which I love to remember and still now am thankful for. After the holidays all the guests departed except for me. Macki and I spent much time together. We rode every day and went to hunt the heathcock. One day Macki proposed to me, and I accepted. Thus we were engaged, but kept it secret for the moment. Macki had to return to the front in several days. For me, Macki was a perfect being, with an angelic, good character. In my isolated youth, where I spent more time with animals than humans, I had learned little about human nature or the ways of the world. I was filled with illusions.

18. Hummelshof Revisited

When I returned to Peddeln it was May 1916, and spring was in full bloom. The loss of Hummelshof remained like an open wound in my heart. I tried to overcome that feeling, but was not able to. I felt that I was without a home. I hesitated for a long time, but one day decided to ride over to Hummelshof. I feared that I would find great changes there, and I was right.

I rode through the woods and came closer and closer to the well-known areas of my childhood. Through the branches of the trees glimmered the old tower; it made me think of those many hours I had spent up there early in the mornings, studying for my exams. Then I approached the avenue leading to the house, lined on each side with enormous, old oaks. How many times did we pass there on foot, or on horseback, or in a carriage. I continued into the courtyard of the house, which had such lovely plantings, trees and lawns. Now it was sadly neglected and no one seemed to be in residence. The house seemed to me cold and soulless as I rode past it. It gave me the shivers. Then I came to the park, which used to be so lovely and well cared for. Now it was overgrowing from neglect. The benches and tables, where we had gathered so often, had disappeared. I saw in my mind the sandbox where I used to play and the big swing where we used to fly through the air. Now everything was silent—no birds to be heard, no friendly dogs wagging their tails, no laughter of children at play.

I continued riding slowly through the large English park into the forest and to our swimming place on the river. How often we had come here in the summers, with the red carriage pulled by ponies. Herr Herbig had taught us to swim, and often we swam quite far. Early spring by the river was unbelievably beautiful, as the ice was melting. The river's waters would overflow its banks, and big chunks of ice would grate against each other. Out of the blue sky came the joyful song of the larks. Yet now it all seemed dead to me. I turned around and with a heavy heart rode back to Peddeln, determined never to return to Hummelshof again.

19. My Trip to the Crimea

For some time now I had been suffering from a chronic bronchial infection. It was the desire of my parents that I see a physician in Dorpat (now Tartu). This doctor, without knowing it, was the cause of a most wonderful adventure and interesting time that enriched my life tremendously. As a cure to my chronic condition, he ordered that I spend several months in Yalta, in the Crimea. At the same time, doctors discovered that Illa, suffering from back pains, had a recurrence of the tuberculosis infection in her spine. She was advised to do a lengthy cure in Yalta. Thus we joined forces, and together we took a sleeping car on the train to St. Petersburg, which was the first stop on our trip.

At the station we were welcomed by Illa's brother Mori. He had a beautifully furnished apartment that he shared with another Guard's officer friend. Macki had already been reassigned to the front. It had a comfortable guest room, where Illa and I stayed. We remained with them for two weeks and were terribly spoiled by the two young men. We had a very interesting and pleasant time, driving around the city in the officers' elegant carriage, looking at all the sites. We saw the famous St. Isaac's Cathedral, with its many icons decorated with precious stones. We heard choirs that sang the wonderful Russian religious songs and went a number of times to the theatre and opera. We walked on the Nevsky Prospekt and saw graceful, elegant ladies with their escorts. We passed by the Winter Palace, and visited the Hermitage art museum. There I saw the paintings of my maternal great-grandfather, Gerhard Christof-Wilhem von Reutern (1791-1865). As *aide-de-camp* to the Russian Field Marshall Prince Barclay de Tolly, this ancestor participated in the battles against Napoleon. He lost his right arm, but in time learned to use his left arm for painting and became very successful at it. He was appointed court painter in 1835. His son, my great uncle, was Michael Count von Reutern, who was Tsar Alexander II's Minister of Finance from 1862 to 1878.

We resumed our travels and went on to Moscow. There Illa was greeted at the station by a friend of hers, Princess Sonja K. (I cannot remember her family name), who had invited Illa to stay with her. Not wishing to intrude on their reunion, I had chosen to be on my own. I had made reservations at a prominent hotel, but when I arrived, I was told that no room was available and that the hotel had already so informed me. Unfortunately, that message had never reached me. I was given the name of several other good hotels, but was warned that there probably would be no vacancies because everything available was occupied by the military. And so it was.

The *izvozchik* (cab driver) drove me from one place to another, without results. Finally, he told me of a hotel where I would surely find a room. We went there, and I was immediately promised a room. First they took my passport, and then they showed me a shabby, dirty room. I was horrified. Fortunately, Sonja had given me her telephone number, and I decided to call her right away. Sonja said she would come immediately because I had landed in a very disreputable part of town. She arrived very soon, but had difficulties with the management, who refused to return my passport. Only when Sonja threatened to call the police did they relent. I was very grateful to her for having gotten me out of that predicament. She took me back to her apartments, where Illa was waiting.

We spent three weeks of our Moscow visit there. Again we did a lot of sightseeing. We visited the Kremlin, the cathedrals, and the fascinating Tretiakovskaia Gallery, which housed the paintings of the great Russian painters, such as Repin, Aivazovskij, Vereshchagin and many others. I returned many times to the Gallery and engrossed myself in these paintings which had so much to say. In one of the rooms was a painting by Repin which occupied the whole room. It was titled "Tsar Ivan the Terrible Murders His Son." This painting was incredibly realistic and full of life. The image would take a hold of one and not let go. It happened once that a student, upon seeing the painting, pulled out a knife and cut it up, screaming, "Enough blood has flowed in Russia. We don't need such pictures!" The painter Repin repaired the painting so well, however, that one cannot notice any of the damage done. I also discovered in one of the cathedrals a boys' choir that sang so angelically that it deeply impressed me. Many other sights were admired by us during those weeks, including the hill outside Moscow, Sparrows Hill, where Napoleon watched the burning of Moscow. Then it was time to continue our trip to Yalta.

Sonja accompanied us. We boarded an international sleeping car, first class, because the trip would take three days and three nights. Illa and Sonja shared a compartment, and I had one to myself. On one side of the large window was a club chair with a table, and on the other side was a sofa and a bed for the night. A sliding door led to a private bathroom. As a precaution, I had brought along a rubber tub and bowl, which came in very useful during my travels. Every day I was able to soap and wash my whole body. Shoes and clothes one could put in front of the door in the evening, and they were returned in the morning after having been cleaned and brushed by the *provodnik* (train steward). There was no dining car, although one could order tea. However, the train stopped long enough in the larger stations that one could have a good meal in the station restaurant.

I spent much time sitting by the window and looking out at the constantly changing panorama. We were crossing Russia from the far north to the deep south. In the north the landscape reminded me of home, with the giant evergreens and forests of scotch pines mixed with birch trees. In Ukraine the landscape changed: for one and a half days and a whole night we were rolling through endless steppes, with scattered herds of cows and horses surrounded by mounted shepherds. In other areas the fertile earth was being tilled with plows pulled by oxen. Now and then one would see a village with white-painted houses and straw roofs, and in the middle, a church. Very early in the morning on the last day of our trip, we passed over the narrow strip of land that connects the Crimean peninsula to the mainland. Before noon we arrived in Simferopol, where we left the train.

From this point on we could only reach Yalta, still eighty kilometers away, by horse or by car. As we looked around, we found ourselves in another world. It was the Orient that greeted us. We saw veiled women, men in turbans and flowing robes. Other men wore bright blue blouses with wide, red sashes. Their faces were darkened by the sun, and their hair and eyes were dark brown. My first thought was that I was living a tale from *A Thousand and One Nights*.

The Crimea is populated by Tatars, and was formerly a part of the Turkish Empire. Russia conquered the territory under the Empress Catherine the Great. Later, under orders from Stalin, the whole Tatar population was forcibly resettled in Siberia. The Tatars follow the teachings of Mohammed; everywhere there were the minarets from the Moslem mosques towering over the houses.

My companions and I decided to take a troika to Yalta rather than a car, so that we could leisurely admire the beautiful landscape. On one side of the road was the Yaila mountain range and on the other the Black Sea. The road was excellent and led us higher and higher. The Black Sea and all its surroundings were of a dream-like beauty. When we arrived in Yalta, we rented a room in a hotel, and then searched for an apartment. We were expecting Nello to join us shortly with her friend Katja and needed a roomy apartment. After we had settled in the hotel, Sonja left for her villa which was several kilometers outside Yalta. We soon found a very pleasant apartment, with a breathtaking view of the Black Sea. Nello and Katja arrived shortly thereafter, and all four of us settled in nicely. We prepared our breakfast and light dinner in the apartment, and the larger noon meal we would have in the hotel next to our apartment. Illa and Nello had to spend much time lying down and were not allowed much activity. In spite of that they were always in good spirits, and we all hoped for the best. The climate was unbelievably beautiful; the air was like champagne.

Nello's friend Katja was an unusual person. She was one of those beings who did everything for others without ever thinking of herself. She was intelligent, well educated, and interested in spiritual matters; in addition to that she was very talented with her hands. Without having been taught, she had built beautiful furniture for herself and her sister, and she had built beehives and an incubator for the hundred or so chickens her family had. Her family originated from the south of Russia and had settled in the Baltics, where her father had bought an estate in the neighborhood of Woiseck. Apart from that, he was also a physician and cared for the families of the area, and Katja would help him out.

When he died, Katja's brother took on the management of the estate. To gain independence, Katja rented a completely neglected mill. It was beautifully situated, but was otherwise useless. With the help of several employees, however, Katja brought the mill into working order, and she built herself a house attached to it. She also built a stable the way it was done traditionally in the south of Russia; that is, out of straw and clay with a thick straw roof. There she housed her collection of poultry and several pigs.

When Katja opened the mill for business, the peasants came from far away to have their grain milled by her, because she was very well liked by everyone. It is no wonder, for she was such a warm-hearted, helpful person, especially in cases of illness. Soon after the beginning of World War II, the Soviets occupied the Baltics as previously agreed to in the Hitler-Stalin Pact of August 1939, which also provided for the division and occupation of Poland by the two powers. More than 200,000 Baltic people fled to the West, but Katja remained behind. Probably she could not separate herself from her beloved mill. I never heard from Katja again, and I fear the worst. That was Katja, a beloved friend and companion. She was for me an unforgettable personality.

During our stay in Yalta, Katja and I undertook many excursions into the surrounding areas, either on foot or riding the local mountain horses. Most of these horses were trained to go on the extremely narrow and dangerous mountain paths and to climb steep passages, which they did as smoothly as cats. One morning we decided to visit a waterfall that plunged from the mountain top into the valley. We arrived at the waterfall early in the morning, and decided to climb the mountain, without a path, and not to quit until we had reached the top. We each had a slice of bread but nothing else to carry. It was so steep that we started our climb on all fours. Now and then we came close to falling—below us was the abyss. Once I lost my footing and was hanging by my arms, but Katja, who was as strong as a man, pulled me up again. After many hours we arrived at the top. There was a flat, steppe-like area covered with snow, but no trees. A freezing wind blew, and we shivered in our summer clothing. In front of us towered the highest peak of the mountain range, the Ai Petri. We would have liked to climb it as well, but the sun was beginning to set. Below us, lights were already blinking in the ocean resorts; darkness comes very swiftly there.

Fortunately, we noticed a footpath that led down the mountain. The descent on the steep path was almost impossible in the dark. We felt our way with our feet. At one point Katja almost fell down a cliff, but I pulled her back. We could hear rocks rolling down the mountain. Our descent was extremely slow. After what seemed to me to be an eternity, we came to a broader path that showed wagon tracks, and the moon had risen, giving us some light. This path brought us to the highway leading to Yalta following the edge of the sea. It was still far to the city, and I was exhausted. Katja, however, still felt fresh and energetic, and to give me courage she hummed a lively march. At one o'clock in the morning we finally arrived in Yalta. The next day, I was so tired I stayed in bed. Katja, however, got up early in the morning in order to participate in a long walking tour.

Katja and I made many other excursions together. One that was quite impressive was a trip on horseback to the ocean resort Alupka. There we visited a castle built in the Tudor style, situated on the edge of the sea. It belonged to the governor, Duke Voronzov-Dashkov. This castle had a renowned terrace leading to the gardens and from there to the sea, all in white marble. A wide marble staircase led down to the formal gardens. Coming from below, one would see on each side of the marble staircase two over-sized, sleeping lions, also in white marble; a little higher were two lions awake with their heads held high; and higher yet, two lions stood furious and threatening. All six lions were masterfully built. Not far from the land there was a giant boulder towering out of the water, waves rushing high against it. This boulder is connected with the mainland by a narrow bridge. On this rock the great painter, Aivazovskij, painted his beautiful seascapes when he was a guest of the governor. Since then, the boulder has been called the Aivazovskij rock.

One day I received a letter from Macki telling me that he was asking for an extended leave in the spring so that we could be married. It would be in the spring of 1917, and nobody suspected the terrible events that were to take place in Russia. My parents and sisters were spending the summer at Peddeln. My sister Jenny, who was then eighteen years old, bought herself a young Siberian Cossack mare from a group of Cossacks passing by. She named it Tsiganka. These horses roam wild in the steppes; they are small, strong and very fast. Jenny was deliriously happy with her pretty, well-built horse.

It was December 1916 when Katja and I began our trip back home. While Illa and Nello had to remain in Yalta since they had not yet fully recovered from their illnesses, the wonderful air of the Crimea had cured my problems. Yalta was about eighty kilometers away from the oriental city of Bakchisaray. There we could catch a train back home. The way to Bakchisaray was over the mountains, so we decided to go on horseback. For all our heavy baggage, which included nine bottles of excellent Crimean wine, we used a pack horse. One morning very early we started the trek, accompanied by a guide who cared for us and the horses. We ascended the mountain on narrow paths, with terrifying abysses and giant boulders all around us. We frequently feared for the heavily loaded pack horse when we were on a particularly narrow passage. Once Katja's horse shied and stood up on its hind legs. It was a moment of terror for us, but the horse calmed down and we continued. Once arrived on the ridge of the mountain, we began the descent.

After some hours, without mishap, we reached the valley and flat ground again. We stopped in a large Tatar village, where the Tatar chief invited us into his house. We were led to a room that was furnished in the European style, with chairs and table, and we were served Turkish coffee. Our host was Moslem, and thus had two wives who served us. The conversation was in Russian. Later he showed us a room where he gave parties. All along the walls were large floor cushions made of silk and stitched in gold, and between them were small, low tables, inlaid with mother of pearl.

Soon we continued on our way. It was a long, tiring ride. We arrived after eleven o'clock at night in Bakchisaray. There we were immediately surrounded by a horde of young men, who very politely offered to help us. They introduced themselves as students of the local *Gymnasium*. Since we did not know where to spend the night we asked them to find us a place to stay. They did this willingly and escorted us to a charming house. An elderly, friendly Tatar woman welcomed us. She gave us a nice, clean room and also brought us food to eat.

The next day we planned to visit the old city right after breakfast. When we left the house, we were greeted by our *Gymnasium* friends, who offered to guide us through the city. First we visited the palace of the former khan. The building and its furnishings were completely oriental. The large salon had ottomans all along the wall, with embroidered, silk cushions. In the middle of the room was a marble basin with a fountain. Through a window with a wooden grating we looked into the courtyard of the harem. There we could see a very large marble basin for bathing, surrounded by columns. It is said that the khan watched the women of his harem from this window. Now all is empty and quiet, and only a fairy tale from *A Thousand and One Nights*. From there we made our way to the colorful market. We saw the most beautiful oriental carpets, embroidered shawls, fabrics, and so on, as well as handmade and intricately hammered silver items. After a few hours we said farewell to our companions and returned to our room, quite tired out.

The next day we ordered a carriage in order to visit Chifut Kalee, which was about six kilometers away. It was an ancient city built by Scythians in the sixth or seventh century B.C. First we arrived at a large, iron door, on which one had to knock loudly with a hammer. A very old man opened the door. He was one of three surviving Koreymen, an old religious sect. He lived there with two other old men, and together they guided visitors around the area.

On the third day we boarded the train. This time our accommodations were not so good because we traveled second class, which was very crowded. As the train moved further north it became colder and colder, and we were freezing in our summer dresses. In Moscow the train stopped for an hour. It was sub-zero weather with deep snow. Then the train continued to St. Petersburg. There we spent a week, going to the theatre, the opera and concerts. When we arrived in the Baltics, we parted ways. Katja went on to Estonia to her father's estate, Loper, and I continued on to Riga where my parents were. I found my parents and sisters well and in good spirits when I arrived. Together we celebrated Christmas; there was much that we had to tell each other.

20. Wedding and Marriage

I heard from Macki that he had been granted the spring leave that he had requested, and we could get married as planned. Time passed very quickly with preparations for the wedding, which was to take place on April 19, 1917, at my parents' apartments in Riga. Macki arrived before the wedding and stayed with a friend, but spent most of his time with us. The German army was still right outside the city. We had grown accustomed to the thunder of cannon and the falling of bombs, and to the thought that any day the city could be attacked. In Russia, the revolution had begun under Alexander Kerensky, without much bloodshed. Kerensky became prime minister, and the Tsar abdicated on March 15, 1917. For me all this had little importance at the time. I was too preoccupied with wedding preparations and my own personal life. How could I have known how much the aftermath of these events would dominate my future and repeatedly put all of our lives in jeopardy!

Our April wedding took place as planned with only our families and close relatives present. We spent our honeymoon in a villa in the Kaiserwald near Riga. Two weeks later we traveled to Woiseck to spend the rest of Macki's leave there. Before leaving, I promised my sister Jenny that, should Riga fall to the Germans, I would save her horse Tsiganka by bringing it from Peddeln to Woiseck, 150 kilometers northeast.

At Woiseck we had two rooms to ourselves on the upper floor. But we did not keep to ourselves, and spent much time with the family. Illa and Nello had also returned home, although Illa was supposed to return to the Crimea in the fall to continue the cure. At Woiseck we noticed nothing of war and revolution. Everything went its old way. My father-in-law, who raised racing horses, had many horses that needed to be ridden. He gave this assignment to us. Macki was also training his own horse for racing, a thoroughbred stallion named Questor. Sometimes this horse behaved like the devil incarnate. He would go totally out of control, with flaming eyes and ears laid back. I usually accompanied Macki on the race horse Ninon. Although she was a very good, reliable horse, she had the unfortunate habit of running out of control, and nothing could hold her back. Everyone had refused to ride her, but, since she needed to be exercised, she was assigned to me. My father-in-law told me laughingly, "Just let her run. She will always run after the stallion." For four kilometers she ran at full gallop. Never had I ridden that fast, and every obstacle in the way she would jump. But I did not enjoy riding the race horses. There was something impersonal about them, and they were only interested in racing.

The summer passed quickly, and Macki's leave was over in the fall. We received the news at this time of the bloody Bolshevik Revolution that had broken out in Russia, and that the Tsar and his family had been taken away to Yekaterinburg, where they were later murdered. We heard that intellectuals, officers, the nobility, and anyone who did not agree with those who were now in power were subject to arrest and torture. The masses were overcome with fear and terror and those who could, fled the land. Illa was back in the Crimea, having managed to make the journey before the revolution broke out in its full fury.

During the summer, the German troops captured Riga, and I remembered my promise to Jenny to save her horse. Thus, I wanted to go to Peddeln as soon as possible to take the horse out of the danger zone. I asked Macki to accompany me, but his leave was up and at that moment he had to depart for the front. I decided to go anyway, even though I knew there might be great danger because of the retreating, demoralized Russian military. Then I had the excellent idea of asking Katja, who was immediately ready to accompany me. The two of us were together again, facing new adventures.

I sent a telegram to the forester and caretaker of Peddeln to announce our arrival, asking him to fetch us at the train station. We arrived after a long journey on a small, local train, but there was no one present to pick us up. Apparently my telegram never arrived. It was ten kilometers to the estate; we had no choice but to walk. When we saw the endless highway before us, we almost lost our courage. As far as we could see, the street was filled with retreating Russian troops. Everything was there, completely mixed up—artillery, cavalry, infantry, and so on. But we had no choice but to start on our way. All went well. Now and then we were asked with laughter whether we were heading for the front. Both soldiers and horses seemed to be exhausted. Finally, in the evening, we arrived. Our house, however, was completely occupied by military troops and there was no room for us. But, in the end, the officers freed one room for us since we were only staying one night. I asked our coachman to have the carriage ready early in the morning, and to tie Tsiganka and another two-year-old mare to the back, and to let her six-month-old colt run behind the carriage. I was hoping to save these three horses.

Thus we began our return to Woiseck. During the day we drove, and nights we spent on various estates of relatives. Thirty kilometers from Woiseck, we were met by Macki who had returned from the front; he was waiting for us with a carriage. When we arrived at the estate, Tsiganka and the other two horses were put into a small, separate stable. The next day Tsiganka was introduced to the many mares and their colts that grazed together on the lawns of the estate. Tsiganka was led out, and the other two horses, trembling, held themselves close to her. As soon as the other mares saw the strange horses, they approached in a gallop. The little Tsiganka, with the long tail that almost reached the ground, proudly turned her back to them and stood there with her head high in the air. Suddenly, one of the mares separated from the group and in full gallop came to the attack. Tsiganka did not move. But hardly had the other horse approached close enough, than she suddenly kicked several times with her hind legs so that the horse pulled back. This scene was repeated several times, as the other mares also attempted to attack Tsiganka. Then suddenly she changed her tactic, and she herself attacked the mares that were standing together. These fled in panic with their little colts. Several times they galloped around the area, and then they stopped and started to graze. With that, Tsiganka and the two young horses had been accepted.

As the Bolshevik Revolution progressed, some things, though hardly noticeable, had changed at Woiseck and in the neighborhood. Something threatening lay in the air. My father-in-law returned one day from a hunt, covered in blood. He told us he had been attacked by two men, who almost murdered him. The doctor had to stitch the wounds on his head, and it was a long time before he completely recovered. From then on I was always worried when Macki went hunting, and it was intolerable for me when he returned later than usual. I tried in vain to overcome these anxieties, telling myself that there was nothing I could do, but to no avail. Since I could think of no solution, I decided that I must listen to my inner voice. I noticed that inside of me something spoke to me but I could not understand it, so I practiced listening through meditation. Gradually the voice inside me became stronger and stronger, and eventually in times of danger this voice left me no peace until I followed it. It turned out later that my inner voice, once I had learned to understand it, always showed me the right way and several times it saved our lives. I am convinced that every human has this ability, if he develops it. Especially in times of danger one is most receptive to it.

One cold day before Christmas, Macki and I went on a sleigh ride on a road which passed snow-covered grain fields on either side. We were bundled up in two layers of fur coats and fur blankets. Macki's beloved French dachshund, Vutzi, was snug by our feet. She had beautiful, silky, short black fur with a brown face. Her stomach was bare and silky. We were trotting along at quite a clip when, all of a sudden, Vutzi jumped out into the deep snow and disappeared. We waited for her for over an hour, calling and calling her—but no Vutzi. Finally, we went home crestfallen, knowing she would perish in the cold. Macki was very attached to this dog, and we returned many times to this same spot during the next few weeks.

A month had passed when we went again to the spot where she had left us. The snow was still everywhere, but what did we see from far off? —a black spot in all that snow! There Vutzi was by the side of the road, round and fat, with long curls on her previously bare stomach, very happily waiting for us. She had always been a diligent mouse hunter and must have scented and eaten the mice in the harvested grain fields that were feeding on the leftover grain.

Christmas 1917 was spent without incident at Woiseck. After the holidays, my father-in-law decided to move to Dorpat with his mistress. Macki and I received an invitation from Mori, who had also spent the holidays at Woiseck, to visit him on his estate, Kerro. Nello had to go to Dorpat for medical treatments and my mother-in-law remained alone on the estate, as Illa was still in the Crimea. We had a wonderful time at Kerro. We were able to forget the war and revolution by doing a lot of skiing and other winter sports. A deep peace seemed to reign over the area.

One day, Mori had to go to the nearby township and was to return in the evening. I was standing at the window when suddenly I saw ten sleds, fully occupied with armed men, pull up in front of the house. I rushed to Macki, who was in the bedroom, and urged him to hide because he was wearing his Imperial officer's uniform and would be in great danger of being shot. There were about a hundred armed men who entered the house. I approached the men, and their leader stepped towards me and warned me that we would be shot if we resisted. He pointed to the bedroom door and asked if there was someone in there. I said, "Yes, my husband." The man then asked if my husband was armed. I said that he was. He found it unwise to enter and went to talk to one of his men. Then all the employees were called into the house and they were informed that the estate was being expropriated, and that the former owner had nothing more to do there.

In the evening Mori returned. Furious, he went into his office where everyone had gathered. He protested and said that he had bought the estate with his own hard-earned money. But it was to no avail. At least for the moment the estate was lost. Later that evening, the three of us sat in the living room discussing the situation. The two men felt that this was a situation that would pass. To me it was clear, however, that we found ourselves in grave danger, that we must leave, and not only leave Kerro, but leave Estonia and flee to the German side. I spoke my mind but the two brothers dismissed my worries. I became more and more restless and worried, and my inner voice became louder. The next day I again tried to convince them that we must flee, but again my warnings were brushed aside. On the third day, however, they decided I was right and made plans to leave. Mori planned to go to Reval (now Tallinn, Estonia) to try to find out about a way through the German-Russian front, while we were to go to Dorpat looking for the same information.

The next day we left Kerro. The coachman brought us to the station, which was very far from the estate and we had to pass through deep snow. After three days in Dorpat, we received a telegram from

Mori asking us to come to Reval. There Mori told us of a way to pass through the front to the German side. In the meantime, Woiseck had also been expropriated. We learned that they had come in the evening, as my mother-in-law and her sons Victor and Arved were eating dinner. Both of the men were in their Imperial Russian uniforms. It was well known that the Bolsheviks shot anyone in a Tsarist officer's uniform without questions asked. Both sons, therefore, jumped out of the window to avoid arrest. Then all the workers of the estate were called together into the house. When everyone had gathered, my mother-in-law appeared, sat down at the piano and said, "First, we will sing." She began to play a hymn and all the workers sang, while there was furious whispering among the Bolsheviks. The next day the coachman drove them to Dorpat.

21. Escape

In Reval, Mori told us that the situation had become critical for us. Members of the nobility and intelligentsia were being arrested, imprisoned, or deported to Siberia. One of our acquaintances had been sent to Siberia with many others, but had managed to escape from the train. The soldiers on the train wanted to punish him for some small thing, so they made him stand by the open window of the moving train with his upper body bare. It was freezing winter weather, and he knew that in only a short time he would freeze to death. He decided then that he would look for an opportunity to jump from the train. When the train slowed down because of a hill, he jumped and landed without injury in the deep snow. The soldiers shot after him, but missed. He ran back along the tracks and soon came to a train guardian's house where he was taken in by a friendly couple. He was given some clothing and hot soup with black bread. It was not safe for him to stay there, so, after he had warmed himself sufficiently, he left, dressed as a peasant. It took him many months to walk back home, which was several thousand kilometers away.

It was decided that we would leave the next day, first by train to Hapsal, a resort on the Baltic Sea, then thirty kilometers on horseback to a fishing village. There a guide was supposed to take us in the night across the frozen sea, past the Russian guards who were equipped with machine guns, to an island that supposedly was in German hands. We separated from Mori and several other young men who had joined him, in order not to draw attention to ourselves. In Hapsal we spent one night in a hotel.

Early the next morning we were to continue by horse and carriage. It was freezing, but there was no snow. During the night, however, there was a snowstorm and the next morning the earth was covered with deep snow. Nevertheless, the carriage was there early in the morning. The trip through the deep snow went much more slowly than anticipated. Late in the afternoon we arrived in the little fishing village. There we went to the house of an old fisherman. He was to take us by horse to a house on the beach about one kilometer from the village.

While we were sitting at the old man's table discussing our plans, the front door opened and several armed soldiers entered. The old fisherman went towards the men. The soldiers asked him who we were, and he told them that we were friends of his son. The room was half dark, and therefore the soldiers did not notice that my husband was wearing the bright red jacket of a Tsarist officer's uniform. The old man came to us and whispered that we must immediately go to the kitchen of his neighbor's house, where someone would lead us away because we were in great danger.

We hurried to the next house, and there another fisherman took us to the stable and harnessed the horse so that we could leave immediately. The house on the beach was only one kilometer away, but to reach it we had to pass a Russian guard post as close as seventy meters. The horse was small and the snow very deep, and, just as we were passing the guard post, the horse sank into the snow up to its back. It had to be unharnessed in order to lead it out of the snow. I asked Macki not to wait, but to go ahead protected by the bushes. This he did. I followed once the horse had been freed and harnessed again to the wagon. At the house on the beach we were hidden in an attic that was unheated. This was a necessary precaution because soldiers frequently stopped at the house. Another snowstorm was raging outside; this time it was in our favor, for it gave us cover. When complete darkness reigned, we began our trek.

Right away we started crossing over the ice of the frozen sea, which was covered with deep layers of snow. The island we were heading for was six kilometers from the mainland. Guardposts had been placed at frequent intervals. Our guide admitted to us that it was not known for sure whether the island was occupied by Germans or by Russians. For us this was a question of life or death! After three hours of walking, our guide suddenly stopped and told us that, because of the snowstorm, he had lost his sense of direction. We were lost and could not continue because before us lay the open sea. He said he could no longer help us and turned around and went back home.

Totally exhausted and frozen I sat down in the snow; I was expecting my first child. The snowstorm continued to blow over and around us. Macki stood for a long time scanning the horizon. At one place the horizon seemed to be a somewhat darker grey than the rest of the sky. We decided to go in that direction. After one hour's walk we indeed recognized the outlines of the island. Now we would learn whether it was occupied by Germans or not. If it was in Russian hands, we were lost. Quietly we stepped on the island. All we saw were trees bending with the wind. Then a sharp voice called in German, "Who is there?" My husband answered, "Refugees from the mainland." The voice demanded, "Come closer!" We approached the guard, who was standing with gun in hand. He said to Macki, "You are a prisoner of war now. Follow me."

He brought us to a warm house and into a room that was filled with sleeping soldiers. The warmth of the room was wonderful. Soon several military personnel arrived. I cannot remember their rank; I was overcome with fatigue. We were led out of the house, and again we had to walk through deep snow to a farmhouse, where we were to spend the night. The next day we were to be sent on with military guards. In the farmhouse, my husband was interrogated about the situation on the mainland. This took a long time, but finally we were led to a warm room with a bed and covers, where we could finally lie down. Only then did it dawn on me that we were saved.

The next morning we had to cross the ice to the next island, about eleven kilometers away. We were brought there by a guard. On this island, I was taken to a small earth hut, occupied by soldiers. I was exhausted. A soldier shared his hot coffee with me, which gave me renewed strength. The officer in charge decided to send us on in a sled pulled by a horse, since he felt that I would not be able to walk the hundreds of kilometers to Arensburg on the island of Oesel.

The German military were helpful towards us wherever we went. A soldier came with a sled and we started on our way. Macki and the soldier went most of the way on foot. We made very slow progress at a walking pace. It took many days. For the nights we were quartered with the military, and in the morning a new sled and horse with another soldier would wait for us. In Arensburg we were given quarters in an old sailors' hotel. It had been set aside for the almost daily arrival of refugees. Among them were also many German soldiers who had escaped from Siberian imprisonment. They had long beards and hair and were dressed like Russian peasants. Macki was no longer considered a prisoner of war. We were visited by German officers and received social invitations.

It was our plan to travel as soon as possible to Riga, which was occupied by the Germans, but because of the frozen sea, no ships were able to cross. Then suddenly the weather warmed up, and the ice melted within three weeks. We managed to find room on the first convoy of ships to Riga. It was a dangerous trip, because the sea was mined. But the voyage went well, except that I was seasick most of the time.

When we arrived in Riga, we looked for a small apartment and found one with acquaintances. After bathing and changing my clothes, I could not wait to go see my parents. My husband had other plans. He owned an estate, Planup, about forty kilometers from Riga. It was in the war zone, and he needed to apply for military permission to go there. When I arrived at my parents' apartment, I was surprised to find a large party taking place. There were ladies in long gowns, German officers, couples were dancing, and there was dinner and champagne. After all I had gone through, this seemed unreal, like a dream.

22. Planup

After receiving permission to travel to Planup, Macki had left right away to prepare the house for my arrival. He took the train to Hinzenberg and from there walked the nine kilometers. It had been a long time since he had had any news from the estate, and he was ready for anything. On his way he saw many deserted farms. Planup was the same. In several of the buildings, military personnel were living. In the main house, Macki found a lot of damage and chaos. The entrance door was missing, and all the window panes were broken. In many places the wooden parquet floor was cut up, and nothing remained of the furniture. Yet we wanted to move in as soon as possible. It took several weeks of work to get the house into livable shape. We bought only the most essential furniture and other necessities that were missing.

At first it was almost impossible to live there. In the whole area there were neither humans nor domestic animals. Therefore, there were no milk products, no eggs, potatoes, or whatnot. We had no horse, and could not go to the little store near the train station to buy a few groceries. It was toward the end of April 1918 and still quite cold, and we froze because there was no wood for the fire. Then Macki was named district commissioner of the county by the Germans. This entitled him to a soldier's ration and held our heads above water, so to speak.

Soon after we had arrived in Riga, the German army had taken Livland (a historic province containing parts of Latvia and Estonia). For many they had come too late, but many others were saved from death and deportation to Siberia. My father-in-law and other landowners moved back to their estates. Peace and quiet had returned. A month later, our life had improved tremendously, for Macki's father was now in a position to help us out. He sent us twenty cows, pigs, sheep, several work horses and two thoroughbreds, which had been Macki's battle horses. Also, as a wedding present from Victor, we received a purebred mare which became my riding horse. Jenny's Tsiganka and the two other mares also came along with the others. In addition, we received potatoes for eating and planting, rye and wheat seeds, flour, and several chickens. Now we could live and make a living! We had several employees, including a good cook. A number of the families who had left the estate because of the war returned, and thus we also had help in the fields.

All was going well, but I intensely missed the company of women. I was surrounded by men—military personnel and the seven secretaries of my husband who helped him in his commissioner work. Even the house guests were only men. Women were not allowed to visit us, because the area had been a military arena until recently, and only military trains were functioning. Women were not given permission by the military to travel.

The summer passed quickly and August was approaching, the month I was expecting my first baby. We hired a midwife to live with us until the birth, because there was no doctor who could have reached us in less than twenty-four hours. On August 18, 1918, I gave birth to a little girl, Ilse. She was blond, had blue eyes, and a tiny, turned-up nose. I was overcome with a joyous feeling and could hardly comprehend that this tiny, rosy bundle was my child.

Soon after the birth I was able to take up riding again. Macki and I spent much time on horseback in the forest, he on his campaign horse and I on the beautiful mare Marscha. Planup was mostly forest, with very little cultivation of fields. But it had been a very valuable property before the war because of the trees which, straight as arrows, reached for the sky. After the war, the forest was decimated. The undergrowth had not been cut, trees had been felled indiscriminately and used for military purposes, and in many places trees lay one over the other, the wood rotting and only useful as firewood.

Toward the end of fall we received disquieting news. It was said that, as a result of the armistice in the West, German troops were pulling back to Germany and Russian troops would be replacing them. One day in December 1918, a closed carriage pulled by four beautiful horses drove into our courtyard, and out came Macki's brother Arved, his wife and their three little children. They had left their estate, Sennen, which was quite a distance east of Planup, because the Bolsheviks had moved very close to that area. The family stayed with us for only one night and the next day went on to Riga. Arved was very anxious to send his family to relatives in Germany, where they would be safe. They tried to talk us into doing the same, because the Bolsheviks could reach Planup in a few days. But Macki could not make up his mind to leave. Arved then told me that he would return the next day to fetch the baby and me and take us to Riga. He felt it was our last chance to get out.

Once more everything would be left behind. It is always the animals that suffer most in times like these; they have to stay behind. For some time already, many abandoned dogs had found their way to Planup. These were beautiful, purebred animals, probably abandoned by their masters who had fled their homes. They would come to us half-starved and were so grateful for the food we gave them. Yet now we would leave as well, and they would be totally abandoned. The day before we left, German troops passed by Planup, on their way back to Germany. The mood of the troops was unpleasant. Some of the soldiers were confirmed

Communists, and the officers were insecure and ready for anything. In the evening Arved arrived. I was very grateful to him for taking the trouble to come back for us. Macki was indecisive and seemed not to be concerned about our safety, but there was no doubt in my mind that we would have fallen into the hands of the Bolsheviks.

The next morning we left. Arved drove the coach himself; he said that we could trust no one now. He was right. The atmosphere around us was one of insecurity and mistrust. No one knew if he would get away alive. The weather was freezing, but in the closed carriage we did not feel it. I held the baby, now four months old, tightly wrapped in my arms.

In Riga we were loaned a lovely apartment by my cousin Felix. He himself volunteered to join the *Landeswehr*, an army that was being formed mostly of men from the Baltic nobility, to defend, along with the Russian White Army, the Baltics and Russia against the Bolsheviks. Several days later Macki arrived in Riga. He had come on foot. While he was still at Planup, the Bolsheviks had arrived and taken over. He had managed to leave the house unnoticed during the night, and, crossing through the park and the forest, had made his way to Riga. The next day he joined the *Landeswehr*. Arved also joined, as well as my father, my brother Rembert, who was only a high school senior, and many, many others. My mother and sisters had left for Germany. Everywhere panic reigned. People were storming the trains, pushing aside the weaker ones. I was alone and felt completely helpless. In addition, it was bitterly cold.

How could I flee with a tiny baby? I decided to stay, even though I knew that it could become terrible for us. But I did not dream then how terrible things really were to become.

Early in January 1919, Macki came to say good-bye. Riga was to be given up without a fight, because the Baltic forces—White Army Guards, *Landeswehr*, and German volunteers—were still forming and were much too weak and untrained to resist the onslaught of the Red Army. In the evening they left the city; even the police stopped functioning. I leaned against the window as Macki rode away, the black silhouette of horse and rider against the setting sun. I was overcome by a feeling of total abandonment, and a terrible fear for my baby took hold of me. Every minute I asked myself: how will little Ilse survive this? This question nagged me as long as we were under Bolshevik occupation.

Later I went outside, leaving the baby with the nurse. It was very cold, and the earth was covered with deep snow. The city was dark; there were no lights, and only the fire of the burning theatre and other buildings lit the sky. Then, out of a dark side street, came an unlit truck. On its floor lay soldiers of the withdrawing German army, rifles held at ready against their cheeks. The prisons were opened, and incredible looting and murdering began. I headed for home in a daze. My soul was as if frozen.

23. Riga Under the Bolsheviks

The day after the Red Army occupied Riga, I went out in the morning to buy groceries. As I turned into the main street, I noticed several men lying in the snow, shot to death. On the other side of the street stood an unusually large, broad-shouldered man, holding a rifle with both hands. His eyes constantly searched up and down the street, apparently looking for new victims. Then I noticed the first occupying Red Army troops. They were mounted on small horses, holding a red flag, and raced past me in full gallop. They were all Siberian Mongols. My first thought was: Asia is overcoming us, and with it will bring barbarism.

Three days later they visited my apartment. There were several men and women, all heavily armed. They confiscated the silver and other objects of value. Everything was searched. The next day others came and continued searching my belongings. This time they took clothing, shoes, sweaters, and so on.

My husband had brought many suits for various occasions back from Germany, which were all hanging in the closet. I was told that they would return the next day to get these, and was warned that everything better be there when they returned. But I immediately decided to try to save some of the items. As soon as they left the house, I asked a young woman whom I knew to help me. She came at night, and we both put on as many of Macki's clothes as we could, each topping it off with one of his coats. We looked like two wandering barrels. I was hoping that we would not run into the porter, for he was a confirmed Communist and had reported us once already. But all went well, and we hurried through the dark side streets to the house of my midwife. There we gave all the clothing to her which she then hid away. Now I was very worried, however, because the closet was noticeably emptier. I was in luck, though, for the man who came had not been there the day before. Without saying a word, he took everything from the closet and left.

Every day more Bolsheviks would come to steal our belongings. The things belonging to Felix they took as well—the silver, the suits, shoes, and other clothing. But the worst for us was the lack of food; not even a crumb of bread was available. The stores were empty. It was part of the tactic of the Bolsheviks to starve the populations under their occupation.

A few days later, when I came home after a futile search for food, I found the apartment occupied by soldiers. They had decided to make it their living quarters, making my life even more difficult. Those in command knew that my husband was fighting against them in the Baltics with the recently formed *Landeswehr*. Many of my relatives were being murdered; my situation was impossible. Living together with the soldiers became so intolerable that I went to the officials to get permission to move, which was granted. When I asked to receive rations of food, since everything had been taken from me, a man screamed at me, "You will get nothing! You can starve together with your child!" The permission to move, it turned out later, saved my life. I was able to hide, and the Bolsheviks lost track of me.

Now the "red terror" began. Countless members of the nobility and the intelligentsia were being arrested. By the thousands they were imprisoned, tortured, murdered, or sent to Siberia. Many were found dead along the highways, where they had fallen exhausted on their way to Siberia. As I searched for new shelter, I found it with a family that lived in a good area. My sister Irene lived with her husband and two little daughters nearby. The husband was working as an architect for the Bolsheviks, so they were safe and had enough to eat. We were given a living room, bed room, and a room for the nurse; we also had kitchen privileges. There we lived in hiding, because I did not report our new address. I heard about a place where a meager soup was given out, and our nurse would go there every day and fetch two bowls of soup. Sometimes she also brought back potato peelings, which I mixed with some flour and baked in a pan without salt, which we did not have. Everything tasted horrible, but it kept us alive. For little Ilse I had nothing else but mother's milk, which was not enough. She would cry for hours with hunger; it broke my heart. There was nothing I could do.

A young woman, Mathilde, had come to me right after the occupation to tell me that she was working for the Cheka, the Soviet secret police, and could no longer do the laundry for me. The next day I received a visit from a stranger in civilian clothes. He had been given the task to warn me that the Bolsheviks had posted a reward of 2000 rubles for my arrest, because my husband and many of my relatives were in the White Army. He left immediately without waiting for my questions. I trembled with fear and terror. What to do now? Where could I possibly go, and what would happen to my baby? This last question absolutely terrified me. A few days later Mathilde came and told me the same thing the stranger had said. Everywhere, she told me, pieces of paper were posted, promising a reward for my arrest. She added that she had no wish to earn that money.

Then I heard about an underground organization that guided people whose lives were in danger through the war front to safety. The leader of this group was known to me by name. He assured me that he would try to do everything he could for me. My situation was further endangered because now all sorts of people, in danger like me, would come to my apartment to discuss the situation. These were fruitless conversations and only endangered us further. One of the occupation rules was that no more than three people at one time were allowed to congregate in one room. We were sometimes as many as fifteen. One day, when my room was filled once more with these desperately endangered people, we heard the Bolsheviks' typical knocking of rifle butts on the front door. Everyone went pale and silent. Without a sound I led several people into my bedroom. We all sat without moving. The door was opened by the owner of the apartment. We could hear them speak, and soon after the soldiers left. We breathed a sigh of relief.

Spring was approaching, but I did not dare take the baby out. I let her sleep by the open window. Once, when the weather was particularly beautiful, I sat with her by the kitchen door in the courtyard of the apartment building. Suddenly, I heard a large window being opened in the building across the way. I looked up and saw a man leaning out of the window, aiming a rifle at us. I remained sitting quietly, looked at him and thought: Let him shoot; then all this will be ended. But suddenly he lowered the rifle and smiled. I have no idea what he meant. Was it a joke, or would he have fired if I had shown fear? But never again did I attempt to bring the baby into the fresh air and sunshine. I myself only went out covered with a large scarf.

One night, at two o'clock in the morning, there was again the familiar knocking with rifle butts on the entrance door below. I went to the window. Overcome with fear and terror, I felt I was going to faint. I lay down on the bed and the faintness passed. Just then the knock came again at our apartment building door. The owner of the building opened the door, and I heard a dull thud and moaning. They have murdered her, I thought, but she had only fainted. Her fainting aroused the suspicion of the soldiers, and they turned the building upside down, without finding anything. Then they came to my quarters. The door was kicked open, and ten men armed to the teeth entered. All fear had left me; I was completely calm. This always happened to me in the face of danger. The leader asked me if I had a telephone; I told him that I did not. They checked for themselves by turning everything over and under. Then he asked if I was hiding any White Guards; again I answered no. They searched the rooms once more, even under the bed. They were already leaving when the leader turned around and asked me where my husband was. This was a very dangerous question and could cost our lives. But I had prepared an answer just for such an occasion. I said that my husband had gone to Moscow to visit his very ill sister. He believed me and left.

Soon a new order was posted by the Bolsheviks that anyone belonging to the nobility had to register. Those who did not comply would be sent to concentration camps or would be shot. In two weeks soldiers would go from house to house to search. I decided not to register, because then they would have me in their trap. Two weeks later, soldiers indeed went from house to house searching for members of the nobility. They also came to our house and asked the porter if any such persons lived in the building. He told them no, even though he knew about me and was putting his own life in danger. That same night he hanged himself. His wife told me that he had been overcome with a panic-like fear.

Another night, a man came alone and interrogated me. To my surprise, he believed everything I told him, perhaps because I was very calm and answered all questions without fear. But I could feel the circle around me closing in. I no longer counted on surviving this ordeal. The terrible fear for my child's life made me half crazy.

One day, when I received the visit of a well-known chief physician of the children's hospital, I asked him to please care for Ilse, in case I should fall into the hands of the Bolsheviks. He promised that he would, which afforded me some relief.

I had reached a state of utter desperation. Forty of our relatives had already been murdered. I no longer dared ask about the fate of anyone. On one of my walks, disguised under the big scarf, I wandered through the street oppressed by my worries. I had realized that there would be no help coming from man. Then suddenly I had a vision:

within me I saw a gigantic arm and hand reaching toward me from the infinite space above, reaching as if to take my hand as a father takes the hand of a child to give it support. It was as if it was saying to me, "Hold steadfast. I am helping you." With this I knew that I had to take the step and free myself from all desire to be helped by man. As I took this step mentally, I thought the ground under me would sink. Yet it became stone hard, like a rock, and supported me. What creature can fight against the spiritual forces that protect us?

24. Liberation

It was now May 1919. On the 22nd day of the month we heard the sound of shots coming from the center of the city. I went outside and asked a passer-by if he knew what the meaning of the shooting was. He had no precise information, but said that he had heard that there was unrest in the city. I thought no more about it and went to my sister's place for a short moment. When I left her and stepped on the street, I thought I was dreaming. Hordes of Red soldiers were filling the streets. They seemed to be fleeing in panic. I had to squeeze myself against the walls of a house in order not to be pulled along with the tide. Once the street had emptied somewhat, I rushed home and went to the window. There were shots nearby. A few Bolsheviks were running past, fear in their faces. The sky was covered with clouds. As the last enemy turned the corner, the wind blew a cloud of dust after them, and then the sun came out.

In the sunshine, walking down the middle of the street, I saw three soldiers of the *Landeswehr* with rifles. I could not believe my eyes. Now, nothing could hold us anymore. Out of all the buildings people stormed into the street, laughing and crying and talking wildly. The soldiers were surrounded by hundreds of people. I stood nearby and would have loved to talk with them, but it was impossible to get through the crowd. To my surprise, one of the men came directly toward me. He was a total stranger to me. He introduced himself, and it turned out he was a member of a well-known Baltic family. He knew me, and told me that when he was at his parents' home in Dorpat, he had often sat on the wall of the garden and watched me in the garden next door, where I had been a guest of their neighbor. He had no news about my husband, but thought he must be all right since he would have heard from Arved, with whom he had fought side by side, if anything had happened to Macki. The city was taken by an advance troop that had pushed ahead of the rest, and the following day the cavalry, to which Macki belonged, arrived.

I decided to go to the Duna River to witness the march of the *Landeswehr* into the city. A bridge more than a kilometer and a half long had to be crossed to get into the city. On my way to the bridge, I saw many corpses lying in the streets. But we were so used to seeing death and horrors by now, it no longer impressed us. As I arrived at the bridge, I saw the liberating troops march into the city. As far as the eye could see, I saw them coming. My father was right in the middle of them. He was wearing a uniform and was standing on a truck with others. Suddenly, I heard my name being called. It came from a small group of dusty, tired soldiers standing to the side. With joy I recognized my brother Rembert and my uncle Paul, my mother's brother. My brother looked terrible. His face was pale and gaunt and his eyes shined with fever. He was very ill. I learned that, in spite of that, he and two of our cousins had pushed ahead of the rest of the troops and occupied the long bridge over the Duna, defending it against attempts by the Bolsheviks to blow it up. It had been the only way into the city, enabling the troops to liberate it. Thousands more would have been murdered without the efforts of these young men.

As I was standing there, an officer approached me and advised me to go home, because the city was not yet safe. The fighting would continue for some time. Immediately, I started on my way home. But in all of the streets through which I had to pass there was fighting. I had to turn around again and again, searching for a way through. Finally I found a way. Once arrived at home, I took my baby in my arms full of joy, because I knew that we were saved and that now she would be able to get all that she needed.

The next day Macki came home. His friends from the squadron brought us piles and piles of food. I could not believe it. Macki could only stay for a short while, because the fighting continued. I had the opportunity to move to another apartment in the same building where my sister lived. The day before I moved, I went to the apartment to look it over once more. The porter gave me the keys. I went in and slowly wandered through the rooms and in the living room I sat down. Suddenly I heard steps coming from the kitchen. The door opened and there stood a man; his looks were terrifying. His collar was turned up; he was unshaven and deathly pale. There were rumors that Bolsheviks were hiding in empty apartments. We looked at each other without saying anything. I was becoming very afraid. Finally, I asked him if he lived here, and he said he did. Shortly after, I left the apartment and brought the keys to the porter and asked him about the man. The porter reassured me and told me the story of this person. He was the son of a Latvian farmer who was waiting for permission to go back to his father's farm. He had met the owner of the apartment in prison where both of them had been placed by the Bolsheviks. While in prison, the owner of the apartment became very ill with typhus, and this young man devoted himself to taking care of the ill man. As a way to express his gratitude, he gave the farmer's son the use of the apartment.

The next day we moved into the new apartment. I assured the young man that he could stay with us as long as he wished and to make himself at home as part of the family. I had no regrets, because he was the best, most tactful and considerate roommate imaginable. He spent much time with little Ilse, fed her and took her on walks in the park. After a few weeks, he received the awaited permission and went home. The nurse that I had engaged since Ilse's birth was getting very old, and I had to let her go. I took over the care of the baby and remained alone in the apartment.

The news from the front was not good. The *Landeswehr* was not strong enough to hold the large city of Riga against the onslaught of the Red Army. The fighting outside the city was grim. One day the city was attacked by artillery fire. Much damage was done in the residential area. I sat with the baby in the living room, prepared for anything. In the middle of the shooting, the doorbell rang. I opened it, and there was Mathilde. She came in and said, "I know that things are very difficult for you, so I have come to help you." With that, she immediately began to fetch water from a nearby well, since the plumbing had long been destroyed by shooting.

Soon after that the door bell rang again. This time it was Macki, totally exhausted, dirty and with his uniform torn. He wanted to take a bath right away and change his clothes. So the good Mathilde carried bucket after bucket of water from the well, which was then heated on the stove in a large basin. Thus we managed to prepare a good bath for Macki. While he bathed, I cleaned his uniform and repaired it. Unfortunately, there was not much time. Macki ate quickly and then rushed off again. Before he left, he told me that the *Landeswehr* could not hold Riga. He asked me to get in touch with the commander of the corps, so that he could take us with the retreating troops in case Riga fell again to the Bolsheviks. This commander was a friend of ours, and he promised me that he would have a soldier fetch us in a wagon should it be necessary.

25. Retreat With the Squadron

A few days later the moment had come to flee. A soldier came with a wagon, as promised, and brought Ilse, Mathilde and myself to the headquarters of the *Landeswehr*. There everything was being prepared for the retreat, and soon the troops began the march. I was given a very comfortable carriage. In front and behind us some of the cavalry rode on beautiful horses; they were all acquaintances of ours. The train of troops stretched a long way; we moved at a walking pace down the streets. It was lovely July weather, without a cloud in the sky. We moved over the Duna Bridge into the suburbs of Riga. There we were to spend the night, while the squadron was fighting on the front. As we were riding slowly through the streets, a friendly, elderly couple came to us and invited us to spend the night in their house. Gratefully I accepted, since I had no idea where I would have spent the night. The couple gave me a room with a large bed and a crib for Ilse, and for Mathilde they also found a place. At two o'clock in the morning there was loud knocking on the door, and a soldier called out, "Get up quickly. We are moving on." I woke up Mathilde and we rushed to get dressed. The night was warm and clear. On the horizon we could see the flashing and hear the thunder of artillery. Thus we continued slowly on our way toward the west.

We rode the whole day, under a cloudless sky; the sun was shining warmly on us. The pale cheeks of little Ilse took on a delicate pink color. She was very cheerful and waved at the soldiers. But with food we did not have much luck. Everywhere we passed, farms were either burned down or abandoned by humans and animals. Nowhere was food to be found. At one point, a young, seventeen-year-old soldier was missing. He had been riding a horse, and suddenly no one could find him. There was a lot of commotion as everyone searched for him. Then we saw him approaching at full gallop with a container in his hand. In it he had milk for the baby. He told us he had searched everywhere, had ridden from one abandoned farm to another, and finally had found an old woman with a cow in the ruins of a house.

That evening we stopped in a small town to spend the night. We found some beds in a private home, and it was heaven to be able to stretch out. In the soldiers' canteen a thick, appetizing soup had been prepared which we were able to share. It was still dark when we began the trek again; we continued through the whole day. Everywhere we were offered the same view: everything had been burned down and abandoned by all living things.

The next night we spent under the stars, near a river. I was still nursing the baby; without that she would probably not have survived. It was a lovely July night. Ilse was sleeping, wrapped up in a blanket, near the campfire. I had stretched out nearby. But I could not sleep. Around the campfire soldiers were sitting and talking. All around me horses were grazing, and on the horizon we continued to see the constant flashing of artillery. The next morning I went to the river with the baby, where we washed and bathed in the warm river water. Mathilde joined us, and together we washed the baby's clothes. Then we went on. Our goal was a larger city, where the troops were to stay for the moment.

When we arrived in the town, we found accommodations and meals in a refugee home that was privately run. But we could not stay there very long, because there was a constant stream of new refugees who needed the space. I did not know where to go. Then one day I met an officer whom I knew and who was in Macki's squadron. I told him of my plight and how I had had no news. He was extremely friendly and invited us to stay on his estate which was further west in Kurland (now western Latvia). After he informed his wife of our impending arrival, we took a train there. He promised me that he would inform Macki of our whereabouts. We were welcomed with much friendliness and all our needs were taken care of in our new temporary home.

Shortly after our arrival there, I finally received news from Macki. He wrote that he would have a week's leave soon and asked that I find some other living quarters, so that we could spend his free time alone together and undisturbed. I was unable to find anything else, but we spent a wonderful time together. I accompanied Macki on a duck hunt on a large lake at the edge of a forest. We also took many walks, or we sat with Ilse in the park. Before returning to the front, Macki wanted to take us to safety in Germany, only we did not know where to go. Just then we received a letter from his father, who had found refuge on an estate in Germany some distance east of Berlin. He wrote us that his host had offered us hospitality as well. This was wonderful news, and we accepted this generosity with much gratitude. I was now expecting my second child, and Ilse had caught a stomach ailment. The medication prescribed by the doctor did not help. I was worried for her and wanted to go to Germany as quickly as possible so that Ilse could have good medical treatment.

I had learned in the meantime that Nello had married Rolf, and Illa, who had been in the Crimea since the outbreak of the Russian Revolution, had become engaged there to a Russian officer, Alfred Count Radzinsky. In 1918, when the German troops left Russia, the White Army could not withstand the Red Army. They did not have enough weapons, munitions, or money. Many of the troops had retreated to the Crimea, accompanied by women and children and thousands of horses. They had hoped to defend the Crimea, but they were unsuccessful. The Red Army broke through, and a terrible massacre followed. Different countries sent ships to save some of the refugees in the Crimea. In April 1919 King George V of England dispatched the battleship *HMS Marlborough* to evacuate his aunt, the Dowager Tsarina Marie (Nicholas II's mother) and some of the Tsar's other relatives. About the same time, Illa and her fiancé and other military personnel managed to save themselves on a Turkish ship. The ship brought them to Turkey, and from there they had traveled to Berlin where they were married.

26. As Refugees in Germany

After a month with our host in Kurland, Macki, Mathilde, Ilse and I left for Germany in September, 1919. The four of us traveled in a slow, irregular train. Everywhere in the Baltic we noticed evidence of the war, where the military had precedence over civilians. We arrived in a German town called Memel at three o'clock in the morning. The next train to Berlin was to leave ten hours later. We searched for a long time for a room in a hotel, and finally found one. Exhausted, we rested there until the departure of our train.

Macki could only stay in Berlin for three days; his leave was ending. We found a nice guest house where we rented two rooms with meals. I took Ilse to see a doctor, but her stomach disorder did not improve. I bought a baby carriage in which she could sit and lie down, and Mathilde took her often out into the fresh air, frequently to the zoo. Macki and I visited Illa and Alfred, with whom we got along very well. After all our struggles, postwar Berlin gave us a great lift. We went out a lot "on the town" and led a carefree life for a few days. But the time passed too quickly. Macki and I had to separate again; this time for a long time.

Our trip to the estate where my father-in-law was staying continued on the train. After several hours, we came to our destination. There a carriage was waiting for us and we were brought to the estate. My heart was warmed by the friendly welcome we received from our host, the von Kleist family. A doctor was immediately summoned to examine Ilse. He prescribed a treatment that right away worked wonders. Her symptoms subsided and her appetite grew. Finally, she had what all children need: quiet and good nutrition. From the bottom of my heart I was thankful and happy. My father-in-law, who had been living with our hosts for some time already, was loved and spoiled by them. He had completely given up his authoritarian behavior, and now was like an old, wonderful grandfather.

There were four daughters in the house, ranging in age from twelve to twenty years, and a seven-year-old son. I especially liked the second youngest daughter, who was seventeen. Her nickname was Moppel. She often came to our rooms and played with the baby. The estate was large and beautiful, and the house was situated in a lovely park. I infrequently had news from Macki. Our letters took a long time to arrive because they had to go via Sweden, since Poland and Lithuania were in the war zone.

My parents were living in Potsdam, near Berlin, in their beautiful villa, which was surrounded by gardens. It was across the street from the park entrance to Frederick the Great's summer palace, Sanssouci. With them lived all of the family, with the exception of Madeleine, who was in London, and me. My father had acquired a liqueur factory that was doing quite well.

In early 1918, my father had bought two villas in Cannstatt, so that my mother and family could be out of danger and near her sister and enjoy the life at the court of King William II of Württemberg. My father, who did not care for life at court, traveled back and forth between the Baltics and Germany as best he could, to fight with the *Landeswehr* and to monitor the situation in general. Soon after the abdication of the old king in late 1918, he transferred the family to Potsdam so that he could be nearer to Berlin and his business interests. My father had always been a shrewd manager of his estates in the Baltic and about every four years had taken a long trip to distant lands, including the Americas and the Far East. In earlier years, he had made investments in Germany and England, as well as in other areas of the world. Some of these undoubtedly sustained my parents after the expropriation in the Baltics until World War II cut off all except his holdings in Germany.

On the estate where we had found refuge we were leading a pleasant life. Ilse made her first attempts at walking. She had gained weight and was much stronger. I was expecting another baby that was due in the spring. Our hosts anticipated the event with pleasure, and we were treated like family members. Mathilde had taken Ilse to her heart. She constantly watched over her, quite jealously in fact, and she took care of me as well. She was more like a mother to me than an employee. Then the moment arrived, and I had to be taken to the hospital in a nearby town. After a long and painful labor, a tiny girl was born. She only weighed three and half pounds. To my surprise the doctor said another baby was coming. It was also a little girl, even smaller, weighing three pounds. I did not dare think about our future. My situation seemed hopeless to me, with three small children, a refugee in a strange land, almost without means of support, and my husband away fighting in the White Army against the Bolsheviks.

My little twins were very ugly. They looked like ancient little creatures, with their thin, wrinkled faces. Their bodies were almost only skin and bones. But they seemed to be healthy, and had a good appetite. I had plenty of milk for them. They grew quickly and were doing wonderfully, and soon a goat had to help out with its milk. Mathilde had much to do now, to take care of us all. I felt weak for a long time after the birth, and seemed to be unable to regain my former strength. Mathilde developed a passionate love for the twins. They were to her like her own children, as was Ilse. With the exception of me, she trusted no one with the children. She could be quite rude if anyone among the employees of the household offered to take care of them so that she could have a rest. Within a few months the twins had developed into healthy, round babies. When the weather was nice, I would go with Moppel and the children for hours into the park. The children were all tanned and full of life. My ugly, little twins, Ljuba and Iris, developed more and more into beautiful children, with white-blond hair, large blue eyes, and even features.

27. Christmas in Riga

Christmas 1920 was approaching. I received a letter from Macki in which he asked me to come to Riga to spend the holidays with him. He pleaded with me to come, saying it would be unbearable should I not be with him. I did not really wish to leave the children at Christmas time, especially as Ilse was old enough to understand. But I also did not want to disappoint Macki, and so wrote him that I was coming.

Traveling to Riga was a dangerous undertaking for a young woman. I had to spend the night in Lithuania which was still at war with

Poland. After an endless, tiring ride in the train, I arrived in Kovno (Kaunas) at eleven o'clock at night. The train did not go any further, and I had to spend the night there. The next morning another train would go to Riga. It so happened that my father was the director of the Baltic Red Cross in Berlin, and he had given me a letter to the Austrian Red Cross in Kovno asking them to take care of me.

At the station in Kovno bitter cold weather awaited me. The station was overrun by soldiers. A train of wounded soldiers was just being unloaded. It was incredible how many soldiers there were everywhere, sleeping on the floor—every inch was taken up by them. In the distance one could hear the thunder of artillery. I made my way through the masses to the station restaurant to ask for directions to the Red Cross. I was told it was very far and should not go alone because the city was filled with soldiers and terrible things happened. But I had no choice and so started on my way. An icy wind blew through the dark, deserted streets; the snow crunched under my feet. Arriving at the Red Cross building, I heard loud laughing and shouting. I gathered all my courage and entered. The great hall was filled with soldiers, as were the upper stories of the building. I showed my letter to the director, who told me that there was no room in the building, but he would find me a place to stay somewhere else.

He called an old woman who was to take me to a certain place. We went through many small, dark streets until we arrived at a large house. There the manager led me through several rooms filled with beds, and explained that they were expecting a group of soldiers at any moment. At the end of one of these large rooms was a small room with three beds. There I was to sleep. In one of the beds was a young woman who immediately told me that she was a Bolshevik and on her way to Russia. Without undressing I stretched out on one of the beds and waited, come what may. Soon after, we could hear the arrival of the soldiers. Our door could not be locked, and now and then a soldier would stick his head through the door, grinning, "Just to see what the young ladies looked like." I could not close an eye that night.

At five in the morning I got up to start the walk back to the station. I had to cross through all those rooms with the sleeping soldiers. After a long march, I reached the station, and soon I was sitting in the train to Riga. I was so looking forward to seeing Macki again, and was hoping that he had left the front already and was waiting for me in Riga. Arrived in Riga, I went straight to the troops' headquarters, but Macki was not there. Instead there was a letter from him. He wrote that he could not be in Riga for Christmas, only afterwards. He said that he had given his Christmas furlough to a fellow officer. I was terribly angered and disappointed when I read this. I felt like turning around right then and there and going back to Germany.

A few days later he arrived, however. But my joy at seeing him was diminished, and I was worried about the children. I had an urge to return. But Macki talked me into staying longer and longer. One day I received a letter from Mathilde, which went something like this: "Dear Madame! You unnatural mother! Ilse is deathly ill and you will probably never see her again. . . etc." I practically went into shock when I read this. I was terribly worried, and the next day I started the trip back.

This time the route would be by ship from the port Libau to Danzig, and not through the war zone. Macki took me to the train station where he met two officers from his former regiment of dragoons. They were on their way to Berlin. He asked them to keep me company during the trip. I was very glad not to be alone with my worries. First we traveled many hours on the train until we arrived in Libau. There we spent the night at a cousin of Macki's. The next day we boarded the ship. There would be no food served on the ship, so everyone had to bring his own. It was a very stormy crossing and most passengers stayed in their cabins. In Danzig we arrived too late to pass through customs and thus had to spend the night on the ship. We were very hungry and wanted to do the one hour train ride to Danzig to have dinner there. We were joined in our adventure by two gentlemen from St. Petersburg. One of them said that he was familiar with Danzig. "In Danzig," he said, "there is a large hotel in which there is a good restaurant, and in addition there are three ballrooms." We did indeed find the restaurant and enjoyed a very good meal. Of course, we began the meal according to Russian custom with *zakuski* and Danzig Goldwasser (a type of liquor containing gold flakes). With that our strength returned, for the sea travel had been exhausting.

Then we went into the ballrooms. We tried out all three and found them equally good. As is the Russian custom, champagne was ordered. All this was fine with me, for it numbed the burning worries inside me. At three in the morning we arrived back on the ship, and, since we were hungry again, we all fetched something to eat from our cabins and ate in one of the salons, surrounded by cabins. One of the gentlemen pointed to a cabin door and said, "I know that in this cabin a woman is sleeping who is one hundred years old." The next morning a friendly, elderly lady came laughingly toward me and said, "I heard that I am supposed to be one hundred years old. Well, I would have loved to join you last night anyway."

In the morning, after passing through German customs, we went to the train station. There we arrived just in time to catch the train to Berlin. Halfway to Berlin, I left the train, saying many good-byes and thank yous to my travel companions. At the station I rang up the estate—my heart was pounding. I spoke with the lady of the house, and she told me about Ilse's illness, but added quickly that she was all well again. This was wonderful news, and I felt an enormous weight falling from me. She also said that she would send someone to the station right away to get me. When I arrived, I found Ilse a little pale, but healthy and in good spirits. And the twins had developed and grown, and looked well nourished.

28. Return to Planup

In the spring of 1921 Macki wrote me that the war had come to an end, and he had resigned his military position. For some time he had been fighting in the Baltic *Landeswehr* along with a British contingent under the leadership of Britain's Lord Harold Alexander (later a field marshall in World War II and British Governor-General of Canada). But the Bolsheviks in Russia had finally prevailed. Estonia, Latvia, and Lithuania had become independent republics. He planned to return to Planup and to fix everything up so that we could join him there. Something inside me told me that this was folly, although I could understand Macki. After these many years of war and separation, he desperately wished for a home for himself and his family. But my inner voice would not leave me in peace. I wrote to Macki and asked him to have patience, to wait until things had normalized more, for until very recently Planup had been in the middle of the war arena. Macki would not listen and wrote back that the house had been remodeled and was ready for us, and there was no reason to wait. Many letters went back and forth like this, and even my host tried to persuade Macki to wait, without success. Finally, I decided to move back to Planup with the children.

Land reform had been enforced in the Baltic states, which were now socialist (but not communist) republics. Without monetary compensation, all land of the Baltic estates had been reduced to one hundred hectares (about 250 acres). But this the former owners had to rent from the government! It was too little to live on, yet too much to abandon. Planup, a timber estate, had sandy earth, and thus never any good harvests. Agricultural products were lowly priced on the market, and the salaries of agricultural workers rose. That was the situation that awaited us.

We arrived in Riga after a lengthy trip by ship to Stettin, and then by train to Riga. Macki picked us up at the station, where we took another train for one hour, and the last nine kilometers were by horse and carriage. Everything looked lovely at Planup. The weather was beautiful, and I hoped that all my worries would prove without basis. The children thrived in the wonderful forest air. Mathilde, who had returned with me, told me one day that she could not get along with Macki, and so she had to give me notice. This was a terrible blow to me, because for the children she was almost irreplaceable. I hired two young girls from Riga after Mathilde left. One of the girls was of no use, for she was more interested in our young agricultural assistant. The other one, however, was very nice and reliable.

Then one day, Ilse became ill. I took her to the hospital where they found that she had dysentery. She had a light case, but I stayed in the hospital with her and shared her room. Several days later Macki arrived at the hospital with the twins. Both had a terrible case of dysentery. The doctors tried everything and nothing helped. Within four days both of the twins died. Now I understood why my inner voice had warned me so strongly against coming back to Planup.

Life continued, nevertheless, but without my two joyful little twins. Our life had become extremely difficult. With the expropriation of our property, the tiny piece of land that was left us could not support the family. We had to work extremely hard physically, almost beyond our strength. My childhood and youth, my whole upbringing, had not prepared me for this. I became repeatedly ill, with heart problems and a liver inflammation which was very painful. We had to carry all our water up a hill from a well. We constantly had to chop wood for our big ovens and stove which used tremendous amounts of wood. All this was done by one female employee and myself. In addition, the children had to be taken care of, as well as the house, the cooking, the garden, the animals, and so on. To top it off, I was expecting another child. Thus, it was with joy that I received an invitation from my parents to spend several months with them at their villa in Potsdam in the spring of 1922, so that my baby could be born there, and I could have the opportunity to recuperate in my parents' home. The three months Ilse and I spent in Potsdam were especially happy times. I gave birth to a son, Herbert, who was a healthy baby with blond hair and big, blue eyes.

In the summer, we returned to Planup. The baby spent almost the whole day sleeping outside in the sun in his little baby carriage. Ilse was also doing well. She had several playmates with whom she had many adventures in the wonderful outdoors. The summer passed, and the work never ended.

29. Accused of Murder

Soon after we had moved back to Planup, the local authorities accused Macki of committing murder. What had happened is as follows: During the war, Macki was ordered to ride to Planup with a patrol to arrest a Bolshevik spy. When they arrived at Planup, this person was not there but they were told where to find him. Macki sent several soldiers to arrest the spy and bring him to headquarters. He himself returned in the company of another officer to Riga. Later the soldiers, returning without the prisoner, explained that he had tried to flee and they had shot him. Macki had never laid eyes on the person in question, and of course pleaded innocent. He named two officers as witnesses. For a long time we heard nothing more about the affair, and thought no more about it. But one day in the fall, Macki received an order to appear in court with the two officers he had named as witnesses. We still did not worry. Macki said as he was leaving, "I won't leave you any money, for I will be back this afternoon."

But he did not return that afternoon; also not the next day. We had no telephone so I sent our agricultural assistant to the station to telephone Macki's lawyer in Riga. There he learned the incredible news that all three officers had been accused and convicted of murder, and had been sentenced to four years of hard labor. Then they had taken them through the streets to the jail, chained to each other with handcuffs. The lawyer added that they were not accepting any bail to free the prisoners temporarily. There was a big outcry in Riga over this conviction. Total strangers sent delicatessen, blankets, pillows, etc. to the prisoners in jail. Large sums of money were offered by private individuals and foreign banks to buy their freedom. But nothing helped.

In the meantime, things were more and more desperate at Planup. I had no money. The lumberjacks came into our kitchen screaming and yelling, demanding to be paid. Suddenly I was the wife of a convicted murderer. I wrote a despairing letter to my father in Potsdam, and described to him our awful situation. He forwarded the letter to my mother who was in London visiting my sister Madeleine. My mother and sister, having read the letter, sat together full of worries and discussed the situation. Just then a visitor was announced; it was an elderly gentleman, a close friend of the family named Richard Tilden-Smith. This man was a very powerful and wealthy industrialist in England and also a member of Parliament. He noticed immediately that the two ladies were depressed and worried. My mother told him about the incredible news they had learned from my letter. Tilden-Smith immediately decided to go to England's Prime Minister Lloyd George to ask for help. I am sure Macki's friendship and war service with Lord Alexander also helped.

Soon thereafter, a diplomatic overture was made by the British government which resulted in the Latvian authorities promising that everything would be set in order. My mother wrote me about this to calm me. Soon after that, I received a telegram from a banker in Libau who asked me to come to his office on a matter concerning my husband. I immediately went there. From the banker I learned that our old family friend in England had given him the authority to give me any sum of money that I needed, even if it were very large. This was an extremely generous offer. I had to calculate very carefully what we needed; because any money that I took we would have to pay back. It was difficult to decide on a sum. What we could earn from Planup was barely enough to keep us alive, let alone to pay back debts. I discussed this with the banker, who was extremely nice and understanding. We agreed that in case a bail would be set for Macki and the other two, money would be available from this offer to pay it. My father had sent me money before my trip to Libau, which I used to live on.

On my return to Riga I decided to visit Macki in jail and give him the good news. The wife of one of the other officers came with me. It was a terribly depressing visit. We approached the large prison complex, surrounded by a tall wall. To get inside, one large iron gate after another was unlocked before us and locked again behind us. Then we were led into the office of a prison official. He greeted us very coldly, and seemed to be in a bad mood. Angrily, he told us that the sending of packages had to stop, for "this is not a hotel!" Of course we could not change this—and would not have changed it if we could—since we did not even know who was sending the packages and food. We told him this, but his mood did not improve.

Then we were led to a waiting room, where there were several guards. They had hardly laid eyes on us, when they started to mock and jeer at us. "Here come the baronesses, the wives of the mighty barons who are murderers." I said nothing, but my companion talked back sharply. Soon after we were led into a side room. There we saw our husbands behind a double-wire screen, watched over by a guard with rifle in hand. We had very little time, only ten minutes. I could hardly see Macki, the wire screens were so dense. In addition, I had to be careful what I said to him, for the guard walked up and down closely behind the two. Quickly and quietly, I told Macki everything. He seemed to be relieved and more hopeful when I left again. Once I returned home, there was nothing more to do but to wait and hope for the best.

Ilse and Herbert were in good health when I returned. Both had been ill with a high fever when I left for Libau. But I had had no choice but to leave them in the care of their nanny. A week later a letter arrived from our lawyer. He wrote that bail had been accepted and gave me the date when the prisoners would be released. I was overjoyed and of course decided to go to Riga for the welcome. Finally the moment came when we were happily reunited. There was a cloud over our happiness, however, because Macki's freedom was temporary, only until the next session of the court. In the evening we all celebrated together. We were full of hope and joy. Fortunately, when the court in Riga came into session, Macki and his two fellow officers were exonerated. With that, a horrible episode in our lives came to an end.

Once back in Planup, life continued as before—a struggle for survival. We had one poor harvest after the other. But the children were doing well. They thrived in the wonderful good air of the country, and they were all well fed. I hired a fourteen-year-old girl to look after the children and to lend me a hand as well. Her name was Alide. She came from a poor Latvian family, who could not support her. She herself still needed a home and family. Before I took her in, I had observed her with the children, and noticed how nice and reasonable she had been with them, and thus decided to hire her. I never regretted this, for this young girl developed into an extraordinary person. I taught her to read, write and speak German. She was an invaluable support to me in the worst of times, and she was very attached to the children.

Years went by. Everything continued as before, with very little improvement in our financial situation. The children were instructed at home by a woman teacher we had hired. I was expecting another baby. Even though everything around me always seemed on the verge of breaking apart, I was filled with the deepest feelings of peace and happiness. One evening in June 1931, my little Gisela was born at Planup with the help of a midwife. She developed marvelously. I nursed her myself and kept her outside in the fresh air from morning to evening, far into the winter. From this she was hardened and never caught a cold.

I had received a small inheritance from the estate of Richard Tilden-Smith, who died in 1931 in England. This kind, generous man, whom I never met, left a similar trust to every member of our family, including my parents. With this inheritance, Rembert, after completing his doctorate in agronomy at Heidelberg University, was able in 1928 to emigrate to Australia, purchase a large tract of land in western Australia near Perth, and to begin pursuing his dream of growing wheat on a large acreage and raising sheep. Gabie, who never married, emigrated to South Africa around the same time, where she lived for many years. When she became ill with cancer, she went to live with Rembert and his lovely English-Australian wife, Sybil. There she died in 1956.

The earnings from my trust were paid to me monthly and became a great help to me. Now I could buy groceries, pay some of the salaries, and dress the children properly. But my marriage was not going well. I began to think about divorce, but continued to hope that things would change. It took several years until I realized that our relationship would not improve, but was only deteriorating. I therefore made up my mind and spoke with Macki about my intentions. He grew very pale but agreed. I hired a lawyer to arrange a divorce of mutual consent, that became legal in 1936. I was given custody of the children, and Macki was ordered to pay a monthly alimony.

30. A New Life Begins

By this time Ilse was seventeen years old. When she finished the *Gymnasium*, she went for one year to Finn, a very good finishing school in Latvia. After that, in 1936 she found a position in Berlin as an au pair with a Jewish family who were friends of my parents. That did not last very long, because the Nazi regime soon banned Aryans working for Jews. She later took courses in office skills, typing and shorthand to enhance her earning abilities. While in Berlin, Ilse met a very nice young physician, whom she later married. Both had to work to earn their living.

My son Herbert, fourteen years old, went to boarding school in the picturesque Latvian town of Wenden. I myself took an apartment in Wenden at the edge of the city, almost in the country. I moved there with Gisela, who was five years old. I found Alide a job in Herbert's school, as I no longer needed her as before, nor could I afford a nanny. I furnished our new home very nicely with the furniture I had, some of which were very good pieces. I felt tremendously relieved—a weight had been taken from me.

We adjusted well to our new home, although I hardly knew anyone in the area, since most of my family had moved to Germany years before. Financially, our situation was very tight. Macki did not send the monthly allowance regularly; but since he was doing very poorly financially, I did not approach him for help and tried to make it on my own. In late 1938, Macki married Margarethe von Sokolowski, a woman of some means. Up until the summer of 1939, Gisela and I spent each summer at Planup so that Gisela could be with her father.

Gisela was an incredible joy to me. We did everything together and took many walks in the nearby forest and by the river. Eventually we met more people and made friends. Herbert came often to visit and brought some of his school friends. I would make coffee and cakes and enjoyed the conversations of the youngsters. The town of Wenden was a delight to me; again and again I discovered something new in it. It was situated in a valley surrounded by forests and mountains.

Nearby on the mountain, in the middle of a park, was the ruin of the Ordensburg, a thirteenth century fortress of the Teutonic Order. During the time of Peter the Great, some of his troops conquered the Baltic provinces, murdering and burning all before them. When they came near Wenden, a part of the population decided to lock themselves in one of the towers of the castle and to blow it up. Only the ruins are left. Some of the walls of the other towers and the castle are still there. A deep sense of peace reigned there, with the birds singing and a quiet whispering passing through the trees as if dead souls were telling of past horrors.

In the summer of 1939 Gisela had finished her first year of school. For the summer holidays we rented a room on the estate Orellen, belonging to my von Campenhausen relatives. Herbert spent the summer at Planup with his father. Gisela and I had two rooms in the old house of the estate. The house had been built in the rococo style, but it was in poor condition. The owners had been expropriated of most of their land and thus did not have the means to keep the house repaired. The only two rooms that were still habitable were the two we had rented. The enormous windows reached almost from ceiling to floor, and gave us a wonderful view of the park. We used the window as a door to the outside, because the way through the large salons and halls to the front door seemed to be too complicated. We spent a quiet, relaxing time there. Every day we went swimming in the large lake nearby. We spent much time with our relatives, and met some of the neighbors who lived on nearby estates.

On September 1st the voice of my cousin woke me. She was calling to me through the open window. She had just heard the news on the radio that Germany had invaded Poland. This was terrible news. I decided that Gisela and I should leave Orellen and return to Wenden the next day. There was no way of knowing how things would develop and affect the Baltics. In Wenden I learned about Germany's secret treaty with the Soviet Union, providing that Germany would not attack the Soviet Union and that the Soviet Union was to be given a free hand in the three Baltic countries, with the two powers splitting up Poland. This worried me even more, for it meant that the Soviets might occupy the Baltics, which would be paramount to death for us.

What was I to do now? How could I save myself and the children? I did not have the means or know of any way to flee. I learned later that, several years earlier, Madeleine in London had tried to arrange for all of us—including our parents in Berlin—to emigrate to England, but we did not see the oncoming danger of war as she did, and then it was too late. On September 3rd Great Britain and France declared war on Germany, honoring their pledge to support the independence of Poland. Europe was once again in my lifetime sinking into the abyss of war, and I knew from experience that our fate would again be determined by world events beyond our control. I thought of those golden days at Hummelshof in my youth and the later struggle for survival amidst the terror of the Bolsheviks. Was that to be repeated, when now I had the responsibility for my children as well? How could we escape?

∞∞

I had three people who coddled and loved me at Planup—my mother, my father and Alide. I loved Alide like another mother. The divorce didn't make sense to me, and I thought my heart was breaking. During those summer months at Planup after we had moved to Wenden, life seemed so normal. Never had I heard my parents quarrel.

And then Papi, whom I adored, remarried. His new wife's nickname is "Mosquito"—but her real name is Margarete. Why "Mosquito"?

Last summer we spent at Planup. Oh! It was so wonderful! I wonder how all the animals are. Are the geese still laying their eggs across from our park on the banks of the river Tumshuppe? Will the horses remember me, and the cows and the chickens? How is my pet chicken, so beautiful in her brown-red feathers? I know Daisy, our English setter, would jump for joy, with all her cute puppies she had last year.

Planup—my home—the familiar white country house on top of a hill. Will I never see you again? From the terrace at the back of the house are steps down to a driveway and then more steps to the fenced-in garden. The stone bench is on the right and a distance from there, bee houses. A straight garden path leads to the river, where it has become a pond for swimming. And then the river runs a ways past our first pasture where horses and cows and sheep and goats bathe and drink the river water. Eventually, the river joins a larger one. From that pasture you walk up a hill to the stables and a courtyard. From there the cattle and horses can be led to other pastures as well. From the stables you walk several hundred feet through an alley to the other side of the house. You have almost made a full circle. Before you get there, you pass through a hedge of lilacs and then you are at the gazebo, which is magical for me.

At the side of the house, when you look right, you see the fenced garden down a little hill; to the left, there is a circular driveway in front of the three-story main house which connects to an ell, a long, old structure which is used as a guesthouse. The driveway leads through tall hedges of lilacs straight past pastures and fields and woods and especially past the huge old oak tree where "Never-Never" and "Puck" live and the little dwarf family—all imaginary beings my mother had created for me. After a while, you come to the Riga highway.

On walks to our mighty oak tree we would leave cookies for our little friends and whatever else I thought we ought to bring. From there we would walk into the woods and look for mushrooms and berries to bring to our cook for dinner. There were lots of wonderful mushrooms and wild strawberries and blueberries when in season. We would always visit a special place in the woods, where mostly fir trees grew. There in the middle of the ancient forest, where the sun shines in, is a grass-green patch of moss, like green velvet. It was really inviting to lie down on, but you had to look out for ants first and sometimes even snakes. After our last summer visit at Planup, "Puck" and "Never-Never" stayed behind, never to be found by me again.

My brother Herbert, nine years older than I, attended a boarding school in Wenden. He would help all he could on the estate during the summer, but our paths rarely crossed except at mealtime. I tried to help, too. Our garden was filled with pink and yellow raspberry bushes in long beds, and also with gooseberries, currants and strawberries. They ripened at different times. We also grew asparagus, green peas, carrots, beets, cabbage, beans, onions, kohlrabi, fennel and other vegetables. The fruit trees bore apples in different varieties, and pears, cherries and plums. I loved the pulling and picking and tried to do my share without getting in anybody else's way. All this produce could be preserved over the winter in the chilly, but well-insulated basement, where there was also a wine cellar.

Our winters were long and cold. We were covered in snow from November until the middle of April. Spring did not hesitate, it came fast and furiously. The great melt does away with the snow in a hurry, and the plants respond accordingly. The excitement and anticipation of spring coming, the flowers rushing up to show their glory, the warming sun pulling us out of our houses, the chorus of the songbirds lending their cheer to the arrival of this great renewal of life—all is almost too much to bear!

Winter was fun, too. At Planup, I remember accompanying my father and brother on a horse-drawn sleigh to look for the perfect Christmas tree on Christmas Eve morning. Then we returned triumphantly and watched the tree being set up immediately in our ballroom in front of a floor-to-ceiling baroque mirror. Now the wax candles were affixed by someone standing on a ladder, and I could help with the lower branches—there were lots of candles on the tree. Next came the gilded garlands of hazelnuts and walnuts and finally colored glass balls and figurines, etc. That accomplished, Herbert and I were banned from that room until we heard my mother play the piano in the ballroom at evening time. We were in my father's study which was several rooms away—all was dark. As the candles were lit, the light became slowly visible through all those rooms. When we heard the piano, we ran to the ballroom and to the piano where my mother was playing "Oh Come All Ye Children," which we all sang, and then "Silent Night, Holy Night."

Our presents were set up unwrapped on card tables. I saw a sleigh leaning against one table. That had to be for me; it was too small for Herbert. My brother got a hunting gun and shells, clothes and books. I received books, too, because we all loved to read, particularly to help us pass through the long winter season. I taught myself to read with Mother's help. She didn't have time to read to me whenever I wanted, so I found a one-page story in Grimm's Fairy Tales. *My mother read it to me several times, while I followed the words in the book. In that manner, I began to memorize some of the words and the spellings and badgered my mother or Alide to help me with those I couldn't figure out. After I conquered that story, I started reading other stories, bothering anyone available to help me when I got stuck.*

But that summer of 1938 was my last contact with Planup, and I had to put those memories in the back of my heart. Back in Wenden, I remember one day I put on my favorite dress and asked my mother's permission to walk to my nearby school with our Scottie, Peter. I wanted to see Alide, who was working there. She was out, so I decided to walk to the park to see the ruins of the 13th century Ordensburg Castle and fortress. My mother had told me how it became a ruin during the time of Tsar Peter the Great, when some of the town's population blew themselves up in one of the towers rather than submit to the invaders. And, as she had said, there was indeed a special peace in the air, with the birds chirping and the old chestnut trees standing guard.

I had stopped before the ruin and was thinking of this story, when something hit the ground near me. I thought a chestnut had fallen and continued my thoughts. Then another hit the ground. My leashed dog acted nervous. So I looked around and saw four or five big Latvian boys half hiding behind trees. I decided to leave the park, first walking and then running, because I was being pelted with hard chestnuts in their hulls and also with some stones. I reached the street with the boys in pursuit. When I got to the corner of the school street, I heard a Latvian women yelling, "Kill her! Kill her!" I ran at top speed into my school. One of the teachers walked me home and told me not to go anywhere alone anymore.

And so, in this manner, at age eight, I was introduced to the world of ethnic and racial hatred. Never before had I heard a word from my family that such divisions existed or that I should look down on anyone. Little did I know what a terrible world awaited us.

∞∞

Ellen von zur Muehlen

Ellen's father, Axel von Samson-Himmelstjerna.

Ellen's mother, Jenny von Samson-Himmelstjerna.

Ellen with one of the family dogs, probably circa 1910.

Hummelshof in 1912 in present day Estonia.

The von zur Mühlen children at Woiseck circa 1912
(front row left to right Ilse, Moritz and Arved; second row left to right Max,
Nelly and Viktor. The fifth brother, Egolf, was taking the picture).

Madeleine von Samson-Himmelstjerna Montagu-Scott in London circa 1912.

Ellen serving in 1914-1915 as an apprentice nurse
in the Red Cross Hospital at Riga after the war had begun.
(From the Peter Scott collection.)

Max (at the end of second row right) and his brother Moritz ("Mori")
(second row, second from left) with other officers in the Life Guards
of Tsarina Alexandra with the Grand Duchesses Anastasia (left)
and Marie (center).
Photo was taken at the Alexander Palace at Tsarskoe Selo
probably the fall of 1915.

Ellen ("Ello") von Samson-Himmelstjerna in 1917,
the year of her marriage to Max ("Macki") von zur Mühlen.

Max von zur Mühlen in 1917.

Woiseck, the manor house on the von zur Mühlen estate
in present day Estonia.

Ellen with daughter Ilse and the twins at Planup in 1920
(the twins died of dysentery in 1921).

Ilse ("Illa") von zur Mühlen and Count Alfred Radzinsky
on their wedding day in Berlin circa 1920.

Axel and Jenny's villa in Potsdam in the 1920s.

From left to right: Ilse, Gisela and Herbert von zur Mühlen at Planup, circa 1933.

Gisela with her beloved nanny, Alide, at Planup in 1935.

Family gathering of Axel and Jenny von Samson-Himmelstjerna with (left to right) daughter Jenny von Cramer; granddaughter Nanuschka von der Osten-Sacken; daughter Irene, Baroness von der Osten-Sacken; and daughter Gabriele von Samson-Himmelstjerna in their Berlin apartment circa 1935.

Rembert von Samson-Himmelstjerna, born in 1900 and the youngest
of eight children, Rembert achieved his dream of owning a large
sheep and wheat farm in western Australia near Perth. He called
his property "Livonia" from the name of the Russian province
where he was born.

Ellen and Gisela on a visit to England in the fall of 1974.

Peddeln in present day Latvia in 1994.

Gisela and daughter Toby Ives with cousin Dunstan Montagu-Scott
in England, 1994.

Hummelshof as it appears today.

Mamutschka enjoying the view of the Trent River
at New Bern in 1971.

31. World War II and Fleeing to Germany

One morning very early a few days later, someone knocked at the door and called out, "Quick, come to the school! Some important information is being given there!" At the school I found many excited people waiting. Then the director of the school told us about an offer made by the German government that any Baltic German who wanted to save himself from the Bolsheviks would be accepted in Germany and resettled in the Warthegau (German-occupied Poland).

Some of those who had to leave behind what little remained of their expropriated estates in the Baltics and were trained agriculturalists, would be placed on estates in occupied Poland, which in many cases had been owned by members of the Polish aristocracy who might even be distant relatives or acquaintances of the Baltic Germans. Of these Polish landowners, some had fled the country at the beginning of the war or for years had been absentee landlords, thus leaving behind neglected farmland which had not been properly cared for or renewed. The overall scheme of the Nazi regime, of course, was to increase agricultural production to help feed the "Greater Reich" and at the same time to provide shelter and a living to the Baltic German refugees.

A number of ships were being sent to the Baltic ports to transport refugees. Almost everyone signed up for this arrangement (close to 100,000 people); a minority stayed behind who saw no danger. Only later, after the Soviet occupation was completed in 1940, did they flee to Germany. Refugee camps were being set up in Riga and also in other Baltic ports. From there the refugees were transported to Germany. The three of us, Herbert, Gisela and I—as well as our little Scottish terrier—were booked on a luxury cruiser. The ship normally had room for 500 passengers, but 3,000 boarded for this trip. Every inch of room was occupied; people simply camped on the floor. Fortunately, the weather was good and no one became ill.

When we arrived in Germany, I was struck by the changes since my last visit in the late 1920s. Because of the war, of course, the military were everywhere. The Nazi swastika flag adorned not only most buildings, but many officials as well on their armbands. But we were safe, at least for the moment!

We were first given a meal in a large hall, and then a train took us through the night to a town called Greifswald. On the way we were given tea and sandwiches at the larger train stations by the German Red Cross. We spent several months in Greifswald where Gisela also attended school. She was often pelted with stony ice balls by some heartless children on her way home from school because she was a refugee and a foreign-born German with a slight Baltic accent. But the same thing had happened to her once in Wenden when some Latvian children pelted and pursued her because she was Baltic German. How cruel children can be at times with each other!

After their time in Greifswald, the Baltic refugees were transported to occupied Poland and there they were to settle. Ilse, who was living in Berlin, was expecting her second baby. Her husband, an army surgeon, had been placed in a military hospital in Poland. I was given permission to move to Berlin because of Ilse's and my parents' residence there. Herbert went to school in Posen (now Poznan), Poland.

32. Our Life in Berlin

Before Gisela and I arrived in Berlin, Ilse's little Joe (Joachim) was born. After a week in the hospital, she returned with the baby to her apartment. There she had a woman who came every day to help with the housework and the children. My parents now also had an apartment in Berlin. A number of years before, they had had to abandon their beautiful villa in Potsdam, because, in order to avoid the inflation-driven, astronomical taxes on the property after World War I, it had been titled in the name of Madeleine, who, as a British citizen, might be taxed less. Later this worked against them, as foreign-owned property was taxed at a premium.

But my parents were quite content in their large, fifth floor apartment in an elegant, old, patrician apartment building on Bayreuther Strasse, just off the Wittenbergplatz in the center of the western part of Berlin. Just around the corner was the large and grand *Kaufhaus des Westens* ("KaDeWe") department store, on a scale similar to Harrods in London. Then further west on the Tauentzienstrasse was the famous Kurfürstendamm (or "Ku'damm"), a wide, elegant shopping and dining boulevard. Also nearby was the great Berlin Zoo. My father delighted in taking eight-year-old Gisela there. They spent many happy hours walking around, observing the animals and the human race interacting. Gisela's deep love for the animal kingdom was fortified here. On their way back to the apartment, they would stop at the Café Kranzler, have hot chocolate, and regale each other with funny stories. My father had a wonderful sense of humor and meant the world to Gisela. They also played a lot of cards. When Gisela started winning, no one was prouder of her than "Apapa." His sunny and warm personality and definite sense for right and wrong gave us all a lot of security.

My sister Irene had an apartment not far from my parents, where she lived with her two daughters, Nanusch and Ljuba. She long before had divorced her architect husband, Theodor Baron von der Osten-Sacken. My sister Jenny, her husband Wilhelm von Cramer, and son Heinz had a nice little house with garden in Eggersdorf, an eastern suburb of Berlin. Jenny had started a very successful dog kennel, specializing in the breeding of champion Scottish terriers. In the same suburb, Jenny found me a small apartment, where I moved with Gisela. The area was beautiful, surrounded by forest, and nearby was a large lake. Gisela went to public school and was able to skip a year. For the time being, the war was not yet very noticeable, except for the shortness of groceries distributed by ration cards.

I was very happy to live so close to my parents, and I visited them as often as possible. Increasingly, one could hear sirens in the night, the signal for people to rush to cellars and bunkers. Then one would hear the explosion of the bombs and would think fearfully of the poor victims. The longer the war lasted, the worse the bombing became. Sometimes whole squadrons of Allied aircraft passed over twice during the nights and dropped uncountable numbers of incendiary and exploding bombs. As time went on, terrible destruction took place in most sections of Berlin.

One night I woke up with a start, apparently because of sirens. I was very afraid and worried. I thought about my parents, who lived in the middle of the city which was now being bombed nightly; they were in great danger. In their old age, they had to go down five flights of stairs in the middle of the night, often twice every night, each carrying a suitcase. And, after the attack, they had to go back up those five flights of stairs. During air raids, the elevators were disengaged. As I lay there thinking about this, and about the future of all of us, I suddenly had a vision. With my inner eye I saw heavy, black clouds which hung deep over me, and then it was as if a hole was being twisted through the cloud mass, and out of this hole came a voice: "God will not abandon you." At that moment the vision disappeared. Now I knew where I stood. I was filled with a deep feeling of peace and a trust in help that would come from the spiritual world. All fear left me and did not return, even though later we would be in terribly dangerous situations.

Two years passed. In July 1942 Ilse's third child, Iris, was born. They were now living in a suburb of Berlin, but there also was the constant danger of bombing attacks. All the children of that area were brought every night into a bunker, where they were taken care of by nurses. Because of the constant danger, Ilse decided to move to the estate of her father in occupied Poland. Later she would move to Prague to be near her husband, Gerhard, who was stationed at a hospital on the eastern front. Contrary to Hitler's promises to the Soviet Union, Germany had invaded the Soviet Union in June 1941.

The war was taking its toll on the population. We knew very little of what the real situation was. Minister of Propaganda Goebbels gave big speeches assuring his countrymen of imminent victory. For our family, of course, it was a mixed bag with Madeleine in England, Gabie in South Africa, and Rembert in Australia—all "enemy" states.

Gisela and I lived quietly by ourselves. We took long walks in the forest and swam in the lake in the summer, always accompanied by our little Scottish terrier. Our little, four-legged friend had the unfortunate habit of wandering off. He would disappear for hours. But, as soon as the sirens sounded, he quickly returned home, and we would find him a trembling, black bundle, sitting by the front door. We also accompanied Jenny on occasion, when she strode through the forest with all of her dogs. She was breeding mostly Scottish terriers and had excellent animals. One of her males was champion of Germany.

Gisela's attendance at school gave me great worries, because of the constant bombing. She was now attending middle school and had to take a train to a nearby town, Strausberg. The commuting took much of her time, and there were times when the sirens sounded and she had no way to find an air raid shelter or safe area.

Gisela had developed an interest in music and theatre. Her cousin Heinz von Cramer, several years older and talented in writing and music, created and gave to her for Christmas a beautiful puppet theatre with all the necessary puppets and scenery changes. After the war, he became quite well known in the European theatrical world, successfully authoring plays and books as well as contemporary operas. Gisela was in heaven. She would enact plays and different parts and then invite her friends to participate. She was a straight "A" student and loved her school.

One day in the summer of 1941 in Eggersdorf, a small group of my fourth grade classmates came by and asked if I wanted to come out and play ball. There was a meadow next to my house where we could play. After a while, we got bored with that and walked back to the road, where an eighteen-year-old retarded girl approached us on her bike. I had had several nice conversations with her in the past, because she drove by my house often. This time, my crowd started taunting her, and I joined in. She then drove right by me and slapped me hard across my face and rode on. I saw the pain in her eyes and her disappointment in me. I got that message completely and have never forgotten it. It taught me compassion, I hope, and to be an independent thinker, or try to be, and not just to "follow the crowd." I don't think I saw her after that, for I desperately wanted to apologize to her.

Across the street from our house lived an older couple with whom I became friends. They lived in a large house with a lovely garden. They knew I liked to read and introduced me to books by Fenimore Cooper and Karl May, among others. I loved those writers. Karl May wrote stories about American Indians and also Balkan adventure stories with much realism and passion.

That same summer when I turned ten years old I had to join the Hitler Youth. Once a week we met at my school in Eggersdorf. We did a lot of projects, like artwork, etc., sort of like the Girl Scouts. Our leader was this lovely, friendly young woman in her early twenties with silky blond hair named Ursula, who had us all mesmerized by her charm and enthusiasm. We all looked forward to being with her and learning something new to make. I don't remember anything particularly "political" that she pounded into our heads. When we returned to Eggersdorf after spending a year in Poland, I tried to see her, but was told that she had left. Later I heard that she had fallen in love with a Polish prisoner of war who worked at her father's coal yard. They both vanished—I don't know how or where to. I fear their fate was not good.

∞∞

33. A Year in Occupied Poland

In the summer of 1943 I was again plagued by my inner voice. It said to me loud and clear that my parents were in terrible danger and had to leave Berlin. I knew it would be very difficult for them to give up their comfortable apartment at their age and move from here to there without a home. But I also knew that I had to listen to my voice. Thus, I went to see my parents with a heavy heart and told them how I felt. But they did not want to hear of leaving; they would rather die than give up their home. Day and night I was being plagued by the voice inside of me. It was practically screaming at me. I tried again and again to convince them to leave, without success. Finally, after two weeks, they decided to follow my advice.

I immediately sent a telegram to my cousin Toni (my German first cousin from Stuttgart) and her Baltic husband Hans Baron von Hahn, who had been resettled on an estate in Poland, asking whether they would be able to take in my parents. The answer was: "Send them immediately." First, all sorts of papers were needed and formalities had to be taken care of before my parents could leave. I wanted to follow in a few days with Gisela, but the bureaucratic paperwork took a little longer than I had expected. My parents arrived safely and had a friendly welcome. Some time later Gisela and I also arrived. Before we went to Toni and Hans, where we all were to spend the rest of the summer, I rented an apartment in a small town near the estate because I wanted to take my parents to live with me. From there Gisela could take the bus to school. We stayed with our relatives until the beginning of the school year and then moved into the apartment.

After having lived there for two months, we heard that the apartment house where my parents had lived in Berlin and the whole neighborhood had been destroyed by bombs—completely razed to the ground. Those who lived there could not save themselves. Even the asphalt on the streets had burned. My parents lost everything stored in their apartment—important papers, their beautiful furniture, and irreplaceable paintings. But their lives had been saved, and they were healthy. I was very happy that they were safe. Life was good to us in Poland. There were no bombings, and we had enough to eat.

Ilse was in Prague, and there she received the terrible news that her husband had been killed when the hospital where he worked on the Russian front was bombed. She decided to stay in Prague for the moment with her three small children. My son Herbert had been drafted into the German Army, and, after a brief training period, was sent to the eastern front. We were completely helpless as all these events took place. The wheel of fortune, ill fortune in this case, just rolled over us like a bulldozer. Before Herbert left for the front, he spent Christmas 1943 with us. I noticed in his attitude that he did not count on surviving. I knew that he was a dissenter about the war, and the Nazis had a reputation for using these people as cannon fodder on the Russian front. Indeed, several months later he was killed. I know that now he is in the spiritual world, and has overcome all the grief of this life on earth.

We lived in the apartment in Poland for one and a half years. My parents seemed to be content. Every day, my old father would go the rather long way to the baker's shop to fetch fresh bread. He loved this walk, and it kept him healthy and full of life. We read many books borrowed from the local library. Gisela took the bus every morning to go to school, and returned late in the afternoon. After school she was able to eat in a home for children, and could do her homework there as well.

In Poland we were visiting our cousin Toni and her husband Hans. The estate they lived on was beautiful, with a manor house in baroque style and a second, smaller but still large house in the same style. This layout was often the case on landed estates, the smaller house built for the older son (usually) and his family, while the parents ran the estate. Later, when the parents retired, they would switch houses with the young couple who now were managing the estate. My grandparents, mother, and I all lived in the smaller house, but our meals were with our relatives.

A very dignified, white-gloved butler served the family table while the meals were prepared below in the large kitchen with several service rooms. The tall and slender cook was reported to be ninety years old. He was a magician with food. He was also a very nice man, and I loved to visit and observe him. He spoke some German, and I was learning a few Polish words. The previous Polish owners of the estate had fled to another country, but the house staff stayed with the estate.

Hans was a good rider. His horse was a golden-brown, fiery stallion. He invited me to learn to ride. I started out in the courtyard of the stables. Apparently, I was a fast learner because after two weeks of daily drilling, I was allowed to ride cross-country with others. I loved it!

After several weeks of riding instruction, I heard that one of my father's older brothers, Arved, lived on an estate not terribly far away and that his new wife was lovely and friendly. She was of German nobility, widowed, and had a thirteen-year-old son who attended a boarding school for boys in Germany during the school year. I developed a burning interest to meet my uncle and his family. I found out exactly where their place was and committed it to memory.

One fine warm morning, I asked if I could go for a ride by myself. Since it was warm, I wore shorts and a sleeveless shirt and started to ride further and further away from "home," towards the villages and small towns near my Uncle Arved's estate. Along the way I stopped and asked field workers or shop owners how to find these places. Everywhere people were helpful. These were Poles. Germany had invaded their country, and I was German and riding alone. Finally, it crossed my rather unsophisticated mind, consumed by a sense of adventure, that I was being foolish. But never mind, I was getting closer and closer to my uncle's home. Finally, I rode into their courtyard and someone sent for my uncle. He arrived, tall and good looking in his riding breeches and shining boots, so elegant and casual. All of a sudden it hit me, what I had done. I was mortified, yet a little bit proud of my accomplishment.

"So who are you?" he asked, not at all in an unfriendly manner.

"I am Gisela. Your brother Macki is my father and Ello, my mother."

"And where did you come from?"

"From Aunt Toni and Uncle Hans' place."

"Did you tell them that you were coming here?" And the questioning went on.

"No, it sort of happened. I really wanted to meet you. I guess I need to let my mother know where I am."

"All right, I shall call them and you can spend the night here. I will explain everything."

By that time, my new aunt had come out of the house trailed by her son. After introductions, she also invited me to spend the night. She was lovely, a little younger than my uncle and full of charm and warmth.

"You must be hungry and thirsty," she said. "Let's go into the house and have some afternoon tea."

My horse was immediately tended to, and over tea and sandwiches I told them all about my "trip." Then the son, nicknamed Kücker, asked me if I would like to see the house and stables and the park. He showed me everything. We also visited "my" horse which was chomping away at some hay and gave me a contented whinny. Dinnertime came, but I had no clothes to change into. My aunt lent me a skirt and blouse and a long night gown for the night. After a delicious dinner, we chatted for a while. Kücker asked me if I would like to get up early the next morning to watch the deer feed on the meadow next to the woods.

"Yes, wonderful, I would love to," was my enthusiastic answer.

"I will wake you up early," said he.

The next morning Kücker opened my door quickly. "Get up right away," he said. "It's almost too late." I jumped out of bed in my aunt's long flannel nightgown, and we quietly went down the steps and barefoot across the park to the edge of the meadow, by now creeping. My cousin peeked through a bush and there in front of us was a deer family grazing on the other side of the meadow. We watched the deer for a while. It was magical! The mist was rising from the ground and the deer scene became clearer. Soon, they slowly turned around and headed majestically into the woods.

When we returned to the house, everyone was still asleep. So I went back to bed to catch some more sleep. Later, when I got up and went downstairs, everyone was already around the breakfast table. Afterwards, Kücker and I went exploring around the estate—we had a lot to talk about. I told him about Latvia and Planup and he told me about his birthplace and his father, who died too young. I knew he missed him a lot, for the same longing for Papi was pulling at my heart.

After lunch, he asked his mother if I could stay longer. My uncle called my mother and she agreed and so did my Uncle Hans. After all, I had one of his horses! I spent a few more days with my hosts and then was invited to stay longer. My mother soon after was driven over to bring me some of my clothes. She stayed for lunch and then took the horse and saddle back with her.

Kücker and I became best friends that summer until I had to return home and he back to school in Germany. He survived the war, and I saw him once again years later in Frankfurt, after which we lost touch with each other.

By the summer's end we moved into our apartment in a small town an hour's bus ride from Lodz, where I attended middle school. I went to a Baltic German school with Baltic teachers, visited a lot with *school friends and sometimes spent the night with them. In the small town where we lived I again had to join the Hitler Youth, which was run by a most unpleasant crowd. There were a number of Nazi fanatics in the group, and the boys were crude and rude. After two meetings, I declared to Mother that I was never going to return there.*

She had to be quite careful how she handled this, because your family could get "black marks" on its Gestapo record for being "anti-Nazi," etc. While they might not have known about Uncle Rembert in Australia and Aunt Gabie in South Africa, they certainly knew about Madeleine in England, for she had made numerous trips to Berlin during the 1930s to visit her parents. My cousin Dunstan Montagu-Scott told me a number of years later that both he and his mother had made trips together and separately to smuggle family silver out of Germany, which was illegal under the Nazi regime, and at times were only a few steps ahead of the Gestapo. In spite of these misgivings, Mother went to the Hitler Youth leadership and told them that I had too long a trip to and from school and too much homework to attend their meetings. They let me off!

I believe that approximately in the second half of 1940 my father had been "given" a nearby estate called Konti, which had belonged to a Polish family. It was near the Polish town of Kutno. Now I could visit him from time to time. I remember him telling me that the estate was only on "loan" and that he never considered it his. I think that, early in the war, he hoped that ultimately Planup would be returned to him, with all its original acreage, and perhaps he might even regain some of the other family places, like Woiseck. After all, he had bought Planup with his own money prior to the beginning of World War I, after his return from his studies in Munich. I think many Baltic Germans probably had this dream, and, of course, as the war progressed, it became quite clear that their "dream" would not come true. They had become mere pawns in Hitler's plans for the subjugation of the east.

The fields at Konti needed to be revitalized by planting soil-improving cover crops, which were then plowed under. My father did that for two years and then looked forward to seeding grains, etc. He also planted around 1500 fruit trees of different varieties, as well as stands of timber. Then cattle, horses, pigs, sheep, geese, turkeys and chickens were brought in to be bred and cared for. He had a Polish manager for the estate, and they worked very well together.

∞∞

34. Back to Berlin

In the fall of 1944 we were visited by some acquaintances who told us that the situation was becoming very serious for us. Apparently, enormous numbers of Soviet troops were gathering on the eastern front in preparation for an advance into Poland. Our friends urged us to leave and to return to Germany. It was a very difficult decision, but we saw the necessity for the move, and my parents also agreed. I wrote to Jenny and asked her to take our parents to live with her in Eggersdorf, the eastern suburb of Berlin, where bombings were infrequent. I had loaned my own apartment in the same suburb to Irene and the girls when I had left. Their apartment was in the center of Berlin and was very unsafe.

I must tell what happened to Irene during this time. After having moved into my apartment, they one day returned to their place in Berlin to save a few more of their belongings. The packing took a long time, so they decided to spend the night. In the middle of the night the sirens sounded, followed immediately by incendiary bombs. The building was hit and was in flames in a matter of seconds. They had no time to dress, but they filled the bathtub with water, soaked blankets in it, and, draped in the wet blankets, they ran through the smoke and terrible heat down the street to the train station. There they took the train to my apartment in the suburbs.

Jenny wrote that she would take our parents and give them the guest room. I put my parents on a train and Jenny was to pick them up at the station in Berlin. I still had a lot of packing to do, and had to send everything to Berlin. Then the day arrived when Gisela, our four-legged friend, and I took the train to Berlin to return to our Eggersdorf apartment. Irene and her daughters moved to a town even further to the east of the city in hopes of being away from the bombings. She had no idea that soon she would flee in panic back to Berlin, along with many others, before the advancing Soviet troops.

In Berlin the bombing was worse than ever. Day and night the sirens were howling. The Allied aircraft came by the hundreds and carpets of bombs rained on the city. Once we observed from our garden several fighter planes as they shot at each other. The blue sky was filled with shining, silver airplanes. Again and again, one or another would crash to the ground. Parachutes would appear and slowly descend with a flyer dangling from it.

One day Gisela had been standing outside watching when she noticed an Allied plane with a plume of smoke trailing behind it. It was circling around going lower and lower, so that she could see the face of the pilot, who was apparently too low to parachute. She waved to him and he waved back—one human being to another—but, soon after, she heard a crash in the distant woods. That experience made a deep impression on her, because she only felt sorrow for the pilot and for the hopelessness of the war. It all seemed like a terrible dream. All around us was a crashing of shots and debris, like arrows, into the ground. We had no fear, however, for death had become our constant companion.

35. Christmas in Prague

Gisela and I received an invitation from Ilse to spend Christmas 1944 with her in Prague. We made the risky trip by train, expecting an air attack at any moment. But nothing happened, and we arrived without incident. Ilse was renting a two-story townhouse with a little garden. There she lived with her three children and a Polish maid. One incident there was memorable. There was a great shortage of heating materials, and so only the living room was heated and all the other rooms were freezing cold. The children did not seem to mind at all and were in good spirits. One day, as I returned from a walk, I saw with horror that on the wooden floor, next to the staircase, a merry little fire was burning. My three-year-old grandson Joe was very busy rushing to the fire with his arms full of paper to keep it going.

In spite of the icy, cold weather, Gisela and I spent much time touring the beautiful old city of Prague. We crossed the river Moldau on the Karlsbridge and climbed the hill to look at the lovely old St. Veitsdom, as well as the ancient castle, the presidential seat. Soon after Christmas, Gisela and I returned to Berlin. Ilse's eventual departure from Prague was supposed to be taken care of by the military authorities, because she was a war widow.

In Berlin the situation had deteriorated even more. Masses of refugees were arriving from the east. It was an unending stream of humanity, some riding in wagons pulled by horses, others on foot pulling little carts. I remember seeing a young boy among them, about thirteen years old, leading a strikingly beautiful Trakehner stallion. Meanwhile Goebbels gave speech after speech assuring a German victory.

Poland had fallen to the Red Army. People fled in panic through icy weather and ice-covered roads. Many made the trek by horse, moving very slowly. Many were overrun by the Russians, taken prisoner or murdered. Indescribable things happened. Macki and his whole family were wiped out from this earth. They had a terrible fate. Only Nello and Ego were allowed to die in peace in the Baltics.

We learned later through the Red Cross that Macki died in a concentration camp in the Soviet Union in 1946. Arved and Mori disappeared without a trace when the Soviets captured Poland. Illa and her second husband, Gori, were at this time with Victor on his estate in Poland. As the Soviet troops were approaching, they decided that Victor's young wife, Birutta, their eight-year-old son and his friend of the same age, as well as Illa and Gori, would take the car and drive ahead to the west, while Victor would follow with the horses and some of the cattle. They were to meet in a certain town.

On their way, those in the car heard the terrible rumors about the advance of the Red Army troops, how the men were shot, the women raped and imprisoned, and the children carried off to the Soviet Union. Terribly worried about Victor, the group made the error of deciding to wait for him in a little town sooner than had been agreed. They did not know that the town was already occupied by the Russians.

As they entered the town, they were greeted by a rain of gun shots. Victor's son was killed immediately. Gori was taken prisoner and disappeared forever. For the women there was no mercy. Victor's frail, young wife, buried her son with her own hands. She died two months later. Illa and the little friend of Victor's son were put into a prison camp. She had been shot in both legs. It was learned from the boy, who was later reunited with his family, that Illa's health rapidly deteriorated. Her back became weaker and weaker, and she was forced to walk on crutches. One day, leaning on her crutches, she slowly went into the snowy forest and never returned. In the meantime, Victor had reached the town that was to be the meeting point. In vain he searched for his family. Later, Victor was also taken prisoner by the Russians and put into a prison camp, where he later died.

Because of his fluency in languages—particularly German, Russian, Latvian and Estonian, although he was also fluent in French and English—my father at age fifty-six was drafted into the German Army in 1944 to be a liaison officer between the German Army and the "Russian Army of Liberation," commanded by General Andrei Vlassov. Vlassov was a Red Army general captured by the Germans early in the war who, because of his strong anti-Communist views, recruited other Russian POWs to fight against the Soviets. After the war he was executed for treason by the Soviets. My father came to believe that all German efforts to gain the support of the Russian people were doomed to failure because of the brutality of the Nazi regime and its racial persecution of Slavs and Jews.

My cousin in Berlin, Bengt von zur Mühlen, and his lovely wife, Irmgard, have for years owned a documentary film company called Chronos Films. She is a relative of General Erich Ludendorf, who, with Field Marshall Paul von Hindenburg (later president of Germany during the Weimar Republic just before and for a while after Hitler came to power), was responsible for the German victory over the Russians at the famous battle of Tannenberg in World War I. Later Ludendorf supported Hitler in the early days of the Nazi movement, but became disillusioned with him before his (Ludendorf's) death in 1937. Bengt and Irmgard and their colleagues—including his identical twin, Max—have produced many documentaries over the years and have won a number of international prizes in the film world, including several Academy Award nominations. In 1992 Bengt, who in his business had built a good working relationship with Soviet authorities over time, dug into the archives of the Soviet KGB which had been opened up after the downfall of the Soviet Union. He found the condemnation and execution report on my father. It is summarized as follows:

"A cavalry captain, Max von zur Mühlen, born in 1888, had been taken prisoner in February 1945 near Poznan, Poland. He was transported to a POW camp at Archangel, in northern Russia. In 1946 he was found guilty of being a 'traitor to Russia' and also was a 'landowner and owner of 300 cattle and 100 horses'."

For these "crimes" he was shot. While it is true that he was a Russian citizen under the Tsar, he became a Latvian citizen when the Baltic states became independent after World War I and he returned to Planup. Later, of course, he was resettled in Poland under the Nazi German scheme of placing former Baltic German landowners on Polish estates. Undoubtedly, the fact that he had fought against the Bolsheviks in several capacities during the Russian Revolution was also a "crime" to the Soviets. According to a German nurse, who was later released from prison, my father, with his language facility, spent much of his time looking after the sick, wounded and dying. For that, too, he may very well have been singled out for execution.

∞∞

36. Fleeing Again

Weeks passed and one day we heard the rumble of artillery for the first time. It was clear to me that the Russians were advancing for their final assault on Berlin and that we must move from Eggersdorf further to the west. Again, my inner voice left me no peace. Jenny said she was ready to leave, but my parents did not want to move again. They wanted to be left in peace. I could understand them well, but it was out of the question that I would leave them behind, alone and helpless.

Completely unexpectedly, Ilse arrived in Berlin one day in March 1945. She had come to take Gisela and me to Prague and from there to go together to Austria, which the Americans were expected to occupy. She had risked her life, flying from Prague to Berlin, in order to save us It was a testament to her cleverness, determination and good contacts that she was even able to obtain passage on an aircraft, as by this time most air travel was reserved for the military. Yet I had to tell her that I could not leave my parents behind. The next day Ilse had to return to Prague to the children, but fortunately missed her plane which was subsequently shot down. She planned to take the train the next day, but again missed the departure. This train was bombed on the way, and once more Ilse's life was saved. Only her third attempt to return succeeded, when she left from Berlin's Tempelhof Airport and flew home to Prague without incident.

Soon after Ilse had left, our house was rocked by artillery shots. I thought it had been German artillery, but the next day I learned that

Soviet shells were landing in the area. The train station and other buildings were burning. We could no longer leave by train. But we had to leave, that I knew. Quickly I packed a few things into our little wagon that was pulled by hand, and Gisela, the dog, and I rushed to my sister's house, while low-flying airplanes shot at us. Jenny was feeding the dogs, and had given no thought to fleeing. Only after I described the situation to her was she ready to come. Her husband refused to go with us—he wanted to join the military. My parents resisted at first, but then decided to go with us. A second little wagon was packed, and we started on our way very slowly because of the age of my parents. It was a totally crazy undertaking, one that seemed to go against all reason; yet I knew it was the right thing to do.

Again and again we were shot at by strafing airplanes, but they missed. After about one-fourth of a kilometer, my parents could walk no further. While we were standing on the edge of the road, a convoy of German military trucks came by and stopped. Jenny asked the officer in charge whether they could take us along. She promised him one of her best young male terriers in return. He agreed to take all of us, including the wagons and four dogs, mine and three of Jenny's best. Jenny had to go back to the kennel to fetch the dogs, and Gisela accompanied her in order to get my father's warm coat which he had forgotten. The dogs that had to be left behind were to be shot by Jenny's husband before he left.

The convoy of trucks was carrying gasoline for the front which had to be delivered, after which they were to return to Berlin. This suited us fine, for we wanted to get to Berlin. Jenny and Gisela returned with the dogs and the coat, and then we got into the trucks. My parents sat in one truck next to the driver. Our wagons were put into a second truck, and the rest of us rode in a third truck. Every truck was carrying large drums filled with gasoline. The convoy of trucks was very long and moved very slowly. It was truly a ride on the edge of death: repeatedly, we were attacked by low-flying fighter planes. Each time the trucks stopped, all the soldiers ran for cover. But we just remained in the truck, calmly leaning on the gasoline drums.

After a long drive, as evening was approaching, we stopped in a little forest to spend the night. It was not long before we were being shot at by artillery. Hurriedly, the trucks continued on their way. It was becoming darker and darker. The fighter planes disappeared, except for a few who were probably keeping an eye on us. Then we reached a large forest, and the convoy stopped to spend the night.

My parents remained in their seats in the truck, and Jenny also stayed in a truck with her dogs. Gisela ran around laughing and playing with the young dog, and I wrapped myself in a blanket and lay down on the earth of the forest. More and more trucks joined the convoy, all filled with gasoline. Soon after, the first fighter planes attacked. Our camp was lit up like daylight by so-called "Christmas tree flares," which floated all around us in the sky. Then the bombs fell, rushing and whistling through the air. The soldiers ran for cover, but we just stayed where we were. This went on the whole night through. I can still see before me the glaringly lit-up tree tops that were swaying quietly in the wind. I felt no fear. My inner voice had led us this way, and I knew that it was the right way.

The night passed without catastrophe. The fighter planes finally disappeared, and the gasoline had been delivered during the night to various areas on the front. The trucks returned empty.

A fine rain had started; it was early morning. The soldiers covered one of the trucks with canvas and placed benches in it. There we were placed with our dogs and little wagons. We were fortunate that we could sit protected from the rain and that the weather shielded us from further attack by aircraft. However, the sound of artillery came closer and then seemed to be all around us.

We started the drive to Berlin. After a while, the commanding officer stopped and telephoned to find out about the military situation. At this point the telephone service was sporadic, and there was now always the chance that a Russian might answer on the other end. It turned out that only one small passage was still open to the city. We continued immediately and, after several hours, reached an inner suburb. There the truck convoy left us. My parents decided to take the subway train, which was still running, to the empty apartment of my Uncle Paul on the Tauentzienstrasse, near their old bombed-out apartment. The rest of us were to follow on foot with the dogs and wagons, about ten kilometers.

After some time we noticed that Jenny's champion dog had walked his paws bloody. We put him on one of the wagons, which he appreciated very much. Then we continued. Russian artillery started again, and several of the houses on our way were hit. This made no impression on us; we had gone through too much. Much worse was the hunger we felt. We had had nothing to eat since we had left Jenny's house. Our ration cards were only good for Eggersdorf, and without ration cards, there was nothing we could buy. Once, when we were resting, a woman leaned out a window and asked us if we would like to come upstairs where she had for each of us a cold, cooked potato. Of course we accepted gladly—it was something to soothe our growling stomachs.

Toward evening we reached my parents. They had settled down in my uncle's apartment. But how it looked there! A bomb had made an enormous hole in the ceiling and the floor; we had a view of the starry sky. There was no time to think things over, however. The sirens sounded and we had to rush down into the cellar. My poor father was desperately exhausted. When we got to the cellar, he sat down on one of the many empty chairs. Right away a woman started yelling at him, "This is my chair. You have no right to sit in it!" I went over to her and explained all that my father had just gone through. She was deeply ashamed and apologized. After the "all clear" siren sounded and everyone went back upstairs, she offered us a room with bed for the night. This was a big help to us. In Uncle Paul's apartment there was only one bed, which my mother used. My father slept in a very comfortable armchair. Because of his heart, he preferred to sleep in a sitting position. For Gisela I arranged a comfortable area on the floor, and Jenny and I slept in the bed offered by our neighbor. Thus we spent the rest of the night without further disturbances.

37. Potsdam Under Soviet Occupation

We decided not to remain in Berlin. There was only one possibility left to leave the city and that was to take the train to Potsdam, southwest of Berlin. All the other train lines had been cut by the advance of the Red Army. It was generally believed that Potsdam would be occupied by the English or Americans. Since my parents and sisters had lived there for many years in their villa across from Sanssouci Park (the summer palace built by Frederick the Great) and had made numerous friends, they were quite willing to go there. The next morning we brought my parents to the station and put them on the train. We rushed back home to follow them with the little wagons and dogs.

When my parents arrived in Potsdam, my mother went to visit an old friend while my father waited at the station. She was warmly welcomed by her friend, who offered the couple a room with balcony and two beds, as well as meals. We were so happy that our parents were taken care of.

In the meantime, when we arrived in Potsdam, we went with our little caravan, dogs, wagons, etc., to see a friend of Jenny's who owned a large house. She was able to give us several rooms on the upper floor under the roof. Thus, we were all housed and happy not to have to hear for a while the thunder of artillery in our immediate vicinity. But finding enough food was an enormous problem. To get a small loaf of bread, we had to stand in a long line of humanity for four hours each time. We soon started to starve and were constantly searching for food.

One early morning I was awakened by the howling of artillery shots which flew close over the roof of our house. I jumped out of bed, calling to Jenny and Gisela to get up immediately, for the next shot could hit the house. We dressed quickly and ran with the dogs down the stairs. Halfway down we heard a deafening crash coming from our rooms upstairs, and a cloud of dust chased after us. We moved into the basement this time, which had been set up as a living room, to the left of which were two bedrooms and to the right a kitchen-dining room combination. All the windows were broken from the artillery shots, and we were greeted by humid, cold air. It was the middle of April 1945.

We arranged ourselves as best we could in our new living quarters. There was no water and nothing to eat. The artillery shots had destroyed the plumbing as well as the electrical wiring. Our situation became critical. The owner of the house had left right after our arrival. On the third floor lived an elderly lady, who now joined us in the basement. She was a wonderful person, full of courage and humor. Her dry jokes kept us laughing through these difficult times.

The first thing we did was to fetch water from a well about three blocks away. Then we went on the search for food. But, without ration cards, there was nothing to be had. Again, I stood for many hours in the breadline, while fighter planes shot at us. We also had to make the terrible decision to destroy the dogs, except for the valuable champion Scottie, because there was no food for them. Jenny undertook the task to have them shot by a soldier. I was so grateful to her, because I could not have done it. The next day again I stood in the breadline. I did not dare to think of my little four-legged friend. When we had said farewell, he had looked at me so sadly, as if to say he would have gladly come with me. After five hours, I came home with the bread. There was no happy greeting from the dogs, and I knew it was all over for them.

Now Potsdam also was under heavy attack by bombs and artillery. Our house was hit several times. Above us it crashed and clanged, the whole house trembling on its foundation. Once, as we stood together in the basement hall, Gisela joyfully put her arms around me and said, "Mommy, now we can both die together." Her great worry at that time was that I might die before her, and she would be left behind all alone. But our time had not yet arrived; we were destined to continue this life. The house, which was very well built, managed to withstand all the attacks.

One evening there was knocking at the door. Several German soldiers asked if they could spend the night in our house, and we gladly gave them a room. That night was terrible. Without a pause, artillery shots rained on our house and the area around us. The whole neighborhood was burning, except our house. Our bedroom faced the street, and during the night a bullet flew several inches above Jenny's head and crashed into the wall. The next morning the soldiers told us that the city had been taken by the Russians, and that they had to give themselves up and deliver their weapons. I felt sorry for these young men, for I knew that a terrible fate might await them.

We had to leave the house to fetch water. At the end of the street we noticed a Soviet tank. We were hoping no one would see us, but the tank did approach and stopped next to us. Two men jumped out of it and spoke to us in good German. They assured us they meant us no harm, but they warned of the regiments that were soon to follow. They said it would be best for us always to stay calm and not to show fear. Then they rolled away in their tank.

I was very worried for Gisela who would be fourteen years old in several months. How could I protect her from the hordes of soldiers who were coming soon? Jenny and I had to search again for food, as there was nothing to eat in the house. Gisela stayed with the elderly lady. Everywhere we went we saw burned-out and shot-up houses. Human corpses and dead animals were lying in the streets—the smell of death hung over the city. In the inner city there was looting, shops were broken open and everything taken; no owners were to be seen. In the grocery stores nothing was to be found; everything had been taken. Then a man showed us a 25-pound package of sugar. Overjoyed, we took it with us.

We rushed back home, terribly worried about Gisela. We were almost across the street from our house, when we were stopped by a Red Army soldier. Shots were flying up and down the street. There was a fight over one house that was still occupied by resisting Germans. I was desperate and terrified for Gisela. I circled the block, but on the other end I was also stopped by soldiers. One Russian officer said it would not take much longer. We waited. The shooting intensified, and the soldiers surrounding the area had to pull back. Finally, I made a decision which can only be considered insane. I said to Jenny, "I can't wait any longer. I am crossing the street." Jenny replied, "I will go, too."

Then something happened so incredible that we could only ask ourselves if our guardian angel was protecting us, or if those who were fighting had some human compassion left, or both. The minute we stepped onto the street, all shooting stopped. We crossed the street and climbed up a wall into the yard of our house. Immediately, the furious shooting recommenced. We found Gisela and the lady well and happy to see us. Nothing had happened to them. They did have a visit from a Russian soldier intent on looting. Gisela, in a most friendly manner, had offered him a seat and asked him to kindly wait until her mother returned home. Ashamed, he soon had left again.

One of those days when the street fighting was still going on and Jenny and I were looking for food, Gisela had ventured out and was standing by the garden gate peeking carefully up and down the street. A young German boy around fourteen or fifteen years old in a well-worn soldier's uniform crouched nearby, with a heavy gun at the ready. He shouted at her to go back into the house. Instead of doing that, Gisela offered him civilian clothes so he could drop his gun and save himself. With that, he pointed the gun at her but thankfully did not shoot, and went on. He was one of the *Volkssturm* ("People's Storm"), a civilian defense force comprised of older men and young boys Hitler had conscripted towards the end of the war to help defend Berlin.

My parents were doing relatively well under the circumstances. They often sat in the sun on their balcony. The fight over Potsdam between Soviet and German troops did not cause much damage where they lived. They were a little outside Potsdam, near the wonderful park of Sanssouci and their old house. With us it was different. We were in constant danger.

One day Red Army soldiers tried to open our front door with kicks of their boots and hammering of rifle butts. I went to the door and opened it, looking into the furious faces of the soldiers. I gave them a friendly greeting in Russian, and immediately their expressions changed into happy grins. Both the sergeant and the ten soldiers said they were extremely happy to be able to speak Russian with someone. They said, "No one can understand us, and everyone is afraid of us." They decided to make their headquarters in our house. I felt very doubtful about the situation and did not know what to think. But it turned out that our new housemates were very nice, decent human beings, who did us no harm. Now and then they even brought us something to eat. Thus, we felt more or less secure. The sergeant sometimes sat with us for some conversation.

Late one evening, at eleven o'clock, one of the soldiers with whom we had frequently talked appeared with a large pot full of aromatic cabbage soup. He banged it on the table in front of us and said, "I am bringing you this soup. In exchange you have to come with me and peel potatoes for our cook. He cannot do the job by himself." Jenny and I gladly accepted and went with the soldier. He brought us through several gardens—because civilians were not allowed on the streets after 9:00 p.m.—until we arrived in the small kitchen of a house. There the cook, without losing many words, set an enormous basket of potatoes in front of us, and we immediately set to work. Soon after we had begun, the door opened and about ten soldiers came in. They sat at the table, pulled out several bottles of vodka and began to drink. We watched them with growing concern and peeled faster and faster, hoping to finish sooner. The soldiers asked us many questions and the atmosphere became lively.

Russians, being very musical, seize on any occasion to sing their beautiful folk songs. This time also, with full lung power, they began to sing. It was more yelling than singing, though. In addition, the air in the small room was becoming intolerable. Finally, the cook placed a large bowl of soup on the table and gave each man a spoon. Since I was seated too far from the table, I was given my own bowl. But Jenny was given only a spoon and had to join the others, who all ate out of the large bowl in the middle of the table. After we had eaten and our stomachs were full, which had not happened for a long time, we began again with the peeling. The soldiers behaved worse and worse, but then the cook yelled at them and threw them out. We breathed a sigh of relief. Until one o'clock in the morning we continued peeling. Then the cook let us go, and we had to find our way through the pitch-black night and the unfamiliar gardens back to our house.

Once home, we found Gisela standing with the guard near the house, tears streaming down her face. The young Mongol, with his narrow eyes and friendly baby face, tried in vain to calm her. When she saw us she ran toward us overjoyed. The poor child had been terribly worried about us.

One day our sergeant came to tell us that the following night, the first of May, Labor Day, would be celebrated by the troops with a lot of alcohol, and that we could be in great danger. He advised us to barricade ourselves in the kitchen for the night. Thus, we set up a little camp in the kitchen on the floor, with the elderly lady in an easy chair. Her wonderful humor kept us laughing in spite of all our worries. Filled with fear we listened for every sound during the night, but all was quiet. All we could hear was the even rhythm of the guard's footsteps. The next day the sergeant arrived with half a bucket full of rice, some vegetables, and a large piece of meat. He asked us to cook a soup for him and his men. The elderly lady volunteered to do the cooking, and the result was a wonderful soup. The soldiers ate very little, however, and the largest portion was left for us. A few days later our protectors left. Now we were again exposed to all sorts of dangers and deprivation.

The garden of our house had become the home of a number of military horses. Several soldiers were always there. They got used to coming into our kitchen, or they leaned through the windows. They were very glad to be able to speak Russian with us. They would tell us about their homes and their life back in the Soviet Union. Now and then a frowning, mistrustful commissar would appear and join the others. Without saying a word, or changing his expression, he would pull out a little notebook and busily start writing.

I had noticed that one of the soldiers never came to chat with us. He kept himself apart and no one spoke with him. One day, when I was alone in the kitchen and no other soldiers were around, he came to the window and began to speak quickly and quietly, "Don't believe what the soldiers are telling you. Life in Russia is terrible. I have worked for a long time on a *kolkhoz* (collective farm). We had to live in huts built of clay and earth, we were never paid, and dressed in rags and were undernourished. When they learned that I was not a Bolshevik, they killed my wife and little daughter and sent me to Siberia. When the war broke out I was sent to the front, and now I am always being observed. If I say or do something they don't like, they will shoot me." I saw the commissar stepping into the garden, and the soldier disappeared like a shadow. I shuddered.

One day an acquaintance appeared at the house to bring us to other living quarters near where our parents were living. This was wonderful news for us, for our present accommodations were becoming more and more intolerable. Quickly we packed all of our belongings into our two little wagons, and off we went. After a long march, we arrived at the house. The owner of the apartment was able to give us two rooms with bath and kitchen privileges. Unfortunately, this woman was extremely unpleasant and a terrible person. She mistreated her father-in-law in the meanest ways. He was old and weak and at her mercy. Once she admonished me furiously because I had given the old man my newspaper to read. "I forbid you to give him the paper. He is not worth it," she screamed. I answered coldly that it was none of her business and gave the poor man the paper. She had offered us the rooms out of fear of the Red Army, for she thought that, since we spoke Russian, we could protect her from them.

When the Soviet troops had marched in, terrible things had happened in this apartment building, as everywhere else. While the residents of the building were in the cellar because of fighter plane attacks, two children had come screaming into the cellar asking to be protected, for their father wanted to kill them. The family lived upstairs in the building. Soon the father came with a revolver in his hand, and he shot the two children. Then he rushed upstairs and shot his wife and himself—all this out of fear of the Russians.

I had placed a bucket of vegetables in the basement after our arrival there. The next morning I went to fetch it and discovered with horror that my hands were covered with blood. I showed this to our landlady, and she told me that a few days before a man had shot himself there, and she had not yet had the time to wipe up the blood.

The war was at last over, with the German surrender to the Allies on May 8, 1945. We all rejoiced that we had come through this awful ordeal alive. From the window of our apartment we could see the house where my parents lived, and we were able to visit them frequently. I decided one day to return to our former home in Eggersdorf to see if there was anything left of our belongings that could be useful to us. I left very early in the morning. There were no trains; Berlin could only be reached by steamboat. To reach the departure point of the boats I had to walk six kilometers. It took many hours before I reached my destination. The area made a terrible, uncomfortable impression. My apartment I found occupied by a family. My suitcases, which I had stored in the coal cellar, had been broken open and plundered. Only a few items were left that I could still use.

I was told that terrible things had happened there. The Russians had lived in the building, and women and young girls, some only ten years old, were raped. Many of these girls had been in Gisela's class at school, and many took their own lives. Jenny's husband had been found shot in the basement of their house. Now I realized why my inner voice had spoken so loudly to me to leave there. Quickly, I packed the few useful things, including my photo album, and rushed back to Potsdam.

Our life in Potsdam was a strenuous fight to keep alive and not die of starvation. With our Soviet-issued ration card we could get nothing more than one and a half pounds of bread per week. Gisela had started school again and was given a meal there. Frequently, we had to send her into the countryside on bicycle to buy or beg vegetables and fruit from the farmers in exchange for silver items. When Jenny and I went, no matter how hard we tried, they refused to sell us any. But it seemed they could not refuse a child. Yet other times she was chased away by farmers and dogs she had to outrun on her rickety bike.

There were many other things we had to do. We had to stand in line for hours to receive a measly bit of lettuce. Wood or coal was unavailable, so we had no choice but to take our little wagon and walk for many kilometers to find wood for cooking. We took great risks, for there were always countless soldiers wandering around. There were other women who also came to fetch wood. Often we heard desperate cries for help from some of them. I never took Gisela with me into the forest, but the fact that we spoke Russian helped us much; we were never harmed.

The husband of the friend with whom my parents were living had been arrested right at the beginning of the Red Army occupation, and disappeared forever. His wife and two grown daughters remained alone. One day my father became ill, but in two days he was well again. But then suddenly my mother fell very ill. She could not tolerate any food. The doctor was unable to help her, and after one week she died. This was a terrible blow for my father. He could not understand that his faithful life's companion was no longer with him.

The burial was three days later. It was a small funeral, with only my father, Gisela, Jenny's son Heinz, and myself there. Jenny herself was very ill at home. We now had my father move in with us and tried to distract him and have him think of other things. He was eighty-three years old and had become very weak from constant undernourishment. As always, our landlady behaved very badly. She told me, red in the face with anger, "I find it infuriating that your father does not get up when I enter the room!" I told her, "He certainly will not get up and there is no reason for him to do so."

Our relentless foraging for food continued. One day we again had nothing to eat in the house, so Jenny and I went from village to village hoping to find something edible that we could buy. We had no success. On one farm the farmer had just arrived with a large wagon full of potatoes. We asked him if he would sell us a few pounds. He refused and went into the house. One of his workers who was standing near us said to us, "These potatoes are going to be sold to the Russians tonight, who will use them to make brandy." Jenny and I were furious. We decided not to ask anymore, but just to take what we could. We were facing starvation. At the next vegetable field we started to pack as much as we could into one of our baskets. Then we went on to a potato field. There we filled another basket, rushing like mad and scared to death that the farmer would catch us. We noticed too late the approach of a truck filled with sacks accompanied by several Red Army soldiers. They all joined us to help and seemed to be in a very good mood. Then we heard the sharp order of a sergeant, "Everyone continue on his way!" As the soldiers left, they told us quickly that the sacks on the truck contained dried potatoes which they are planning to dump on the meadow nearby. We were welcome to take them all. This was like a beam of light in our desperate situation. We decided to go there early the next morning with our little wagon and to take as much as possible.

At five o'clock the next morning we started, for it was a long way. When we arrived at the meadow, we were only able to load one of the sacks; they were incredibly heavy. It took all our strength to pull the wagon over the soft meadow. Once we reached the hard surface of the street, it was easier. With many rests we succeeded. At home we still had the task of dragging the sack up four flights of stairs to our apartment, but with Gisela's help we managed step by step. When we opened the sack we were disappointed. It contained stone-hard potato pieces, some even burned. For those who had enough to eat they were not palatable. That is why the Russians had thrown them away. But it saved us from dying of starvation. We soaked the potatoes in the evening, and in the morning put them through a meat grinder and then cooked them in water without salt, which we did not have and could not buy. It tasted awful, but it filled the stomach.

Another day we ran out of wood for the fire, so Jenny and I had to go to the woods to find some. On our way we passed a little house. Standing in front of it were about thirty German prisoners of war. Red Army soldiers were running all excited in and out of the house. We had only gone a little further when we heard several rounds of shots and saw with horror that the prisoners had been shot. Trembling, we continued on our way deep into the woods. There we noticed a strong smell of corpses. On the ground we saw a pile of letters and photos, sent by relatives to German soldiers. Next to this the corpses were buried, so shallowly that parts of the bodies were visible.

Jenny and I ran away, horrified and sickened. We finally found a place that had a lot of young, dead trees. We quickly began to gather as much wood as we could, not looking left or right. Suddenly three Russian soldiers stood in front of us. Cold terror overcame me, but I started to talk with them calmly, all the while continuing to gather wood. After a while, they left us and went to another woman and young girl who were also collecting wood. We felt somewhat safer and thought they would not come back. We continued our work, rushing like mad, and were almost finished when the three soldiers returned. Jenny became pale as death. I gathered all my strength to remain calm and said to them. "We are in a great hurry. Our husbands, who are near, are waiting for us." Apparently they believed us, for they did not follow us.

Then there came an order from the Soviets that every person had to report to the employment office twice a week at seven o'clock in the morning and work without pay and food for the whole day. In our half-starved condition this was almost beyond our strength. I especially remember one day—it still makes me shudder. Surrounded by armed soldiers, I was marching with about twenty other women for several kilometers to a place where we had to tear up the cobbled street. The heavy stones were carried by us on stretchers, and then we had to break up the solid gravel underneath with iron bars. At noon we were allowed to pause; a large kettle of soup was brought. We were exhausted and starving, and we all thought we were going to get something to eat. But no such luck. Our guards ate, sitting next to us, and they ate well. We only were allowed to watch. Incensed as I was, I later told them what I thought. The soldiers apologized and said they were only following orders. Then the work continued until eight o'clock at night.

Jenny had started breeding dogs again and had reported that as her occupation. As a result she received an exemption from the work gangs. Later she listed me as her assistant, and from then on I was also spared laboring for the Russians. I would not have survived the ordeal much longer, for I had become considerably weaker. We were half-starved, thought only of food, and talked of nothing but food.

One day Jenny's eighteen-year-old son Heinz came to live with us, having been released from the army. For him we had to find food as well. Jenny and I did not know what else to do but to go to the harvested fields and collect wheat that had been left. We had a backpack into which we put the wheat. Now and then a Russian field policeman would cycle by without paying any attention to us. Then came a car with a Russian commissar and an armed woman. They stopped and forbad us to collect the wheat. We had only filled half of our backpack. But we remembered that we had seen a large, neglected cabbage field. We went there, and after we had cut only one cabbage and put it into the sack, we were stopped by an armed soldier.

From another direction came a German policeman swearing loudly at us and from a third direction came a Russian field policeman on bicycle. There we stood surrounded by these men. The German policeman yelled at us, "You are stealing. You have to come to the *Kommandantur*." That would have meant many days of hard labor, and our father and the two children would have starved to death in the meantime. I explained this to him and the two Russians. But the German continued to scream at us. "That makes no difference!" he yelled, "You have been stealing. First you have to pay three marks, and then you have to go to the *Kommandantur*." Suddenly the Russian field policeman said, "I will pay the money. Let the women go." The German had no choice but to let us go, and we went home hardly believing in our luck. The Russian soldier accompanied us part of the way and said, "That was pretty stupid of you. You should come in the evening when no one is here and you can take what you want." But we did not have the courage to return a second time.

Heinz found a job in Berlin, and he and Jenny moved there. For my father we found a good, Baltic nursing home in Berlin. The woman who directed the home had been a friend of my parents for years. A year or so later Madeleine arranged for our father to be transferred to her home in England, where he died in 1950.

Left by myself, I did not have the strength and courage to find food and wood. I needed a way out. The British occupying forces were arranging trains for refugees who wished to go to the British sector of Germany. I tried to get the necessary papers to take one of these trains with Gisela, but I repeatedly failed. By this time I weighed only 100 pounds instead of my former 135, and I knew I could not last longer than another week. Gisela was doing better; in spite of everything, she was healthy and strong.

Then something very strange happened. I can only explain that it must have been spiritual forces that came to our aid. For some reason we were destined to continue living. At four o'clock one November morning I woke up and was immediately wide awake. I suddenly knew exactly where I had to go and what I had to say to get the travel permission that I needed to get the tickets for the refugee train to the British sector. Terribly excited, I woke Gisela up and told her that I was leaving right away on the long trip to Berlin in order to reach it in time to get the travel permits. Once in Berlin, everything went smoothly; in a few minutes I received the necessary papers. I was told that this train would be the last one for a long time to transport refugees to the West, and that it was leaving the next day from the British sector of Berlin.

38. Our Flight Continues

Overjoyed, I went back home to start packing. The next day Gisela and I went to take a steamboat to Berlin, using one of the little wagons for our baggage. In Berlin we took the subway to the designated train station. There, all the refugees were first given a bowl of thick, warm soup. Then we were assigned a place in one of the train cars, which had formerly been used for cattle transport. We sat on our baggage because there were no benches. We traveled through the night. At one station the door of our train wagon was opened by several armed Red Army soldiers who pushed their way into the car with the purpose of looting the passengers' belongings. But several warning shots from the British guards chased them away. In the course of the next day, we reached the British zone. We left the train and had a medical examination. Then we were led into a large hall covered with straw, where we spent the night. Before that, we were given a bowl of thin vegetable soup. A feeling of tremendous relief came over us, and we felt safe, even though our future was very uncertain.

The next day, our journey continued in the fully occupied refugee train. I had decided to stop in Göttingen where my father had a cousin and good friend who had lived there for many years. I wanted to ask him for advice. All this time I continually worried about Ilse and her children. I had had no news from them and did not know whether she had been able to leave Prague before the Red Army came and to save herself and the children. All my inquires in Potsdam had come to nothing.

When we arrived in Göttingen, we went on foot, weak and hungry, the long way to my cousin's house, carrying our baggage. At his house, we were told that he was very ill with pneumonia and could not have visitors. So we started on our way to a refugee camp outside the city, but the long walk was in vain. There was nothing to eat there. Without ration cards nothing could be bought, and they were only given to registered residents. On our way to the camp, I had seen a sign that said: "Meals for refugees." We went there, but again there was nothing to eat.

It was December 1945 and freezing cold, with snow. We had nothing to eat, no place to go, and night was approaching. I was overcome with the anguished thought that we were going to die there on the street. Gisela started to cry bitter tears. Then she said, "I am going to see my classmate," and she ran off. She was referring to a little girl, Ragni Hasselblatt, who had gone to Poland with her parents and then they had come to Göttingen. I did not know the parents, but I knew their address.

Slowly, dragging our baggage, I followed after Gisela. When I arrived there, I was warmly welcomed by the mother. She told me that Gisela had eaten and was already asleep. I was given something to eat as well, and I was able to take a bath, lie down and rest. In the evening I got up to talk with the parents about our situation. They told me that, as refugees, we could only be given shelter and food through official channels in a refugee camp. The next morning a refugee train was going to the camp where we should present ourselves for aid. Our generous hosts gave us coffee and breakfast the next morning, and some dry bread for the trip. I was very grateful to them, especially knowing that they hardly had enough to eat themselves.

After several hours on the train, we reached the refugee camp. It had become very cold, and a snowstorm was beating down on us. There was a long line of refugees in front of a house waiting to register. We waited for three hours, frozen to the bone, with the snow and wind blowing around us. It started to get dark and we had not yet eaten. The piece of bread that we still had revived us and kept us going. Finally, after we had registered, we were led to a large, former cow stable. Every person was given a bowl of soup. After that, we were taken to the train station, where shortly we were to take a train. The unlit train had hardly come to a halt when the many refugees rushed to get on it. I was terribly afraid of losing Gisela, but she fought her way through and reached the car in time. We were greeted by an icy cold draft, for all the windows were broken. Again, we had to sit on the floor as there were no benches. As soon as the train started to move, the cold increased from the draft coming through the windows. The car was unheated, so there was no escaping the cold. The train rattled on through the whole night. We were literally frozen to the bones. In addition, we were tortured by constant hunger pangs and feelings of weakness. It is a wonder that we survived.

At six in the morning the train stopped for some time at a station. Across from us was a British military train. In it the passengers were sitting in upholstered seats, and we could see how warm they were. Suddenly they noticed our train, with the broken windows and all the refugees. They came out and handed us sandwiches through the windows. We all received two sandwiches; we were grateful to them from the bottom of our hearts. After a while, the train trip continued, and only in the afternoon did we reach the next and our last refugee camp. We were taken to the camp from the station in closed trucks. Then we had to wait again in line outside in the freezing temperatures for several hours. After the registration, we were taken to a large barn, the floor covered with straw. There it was relatively warm, for all the people helped warm the room and there was also a small stove with a fire. It was not until evening that we received our first meal of the day. The next day the journey continued—we had no idea to where. The whole day we traveled until the evening; when it was already dark, we reached a suburb of Hamburg. There we left the train and were directed to a large dining hall, which soon was filled with refugees. After everyone was seated, we were served bowls of thick, pea soup with beef. It was again our first meal that day. Gisela ate with good appetite and went to refill her bowl. But my appetite had gone. I could hardly eat, and I felt ill.

After the meal we were loaded into trucks which drove us for six kilometers to a small village called Hamwarde. There we were distributed among the farmers. Our farmer's wife received us in a friendly way. But she told us that her house was already overflowing with refugees, and she could only give us a room through which other refugees had to pass.

The sight of this room was enough to rob one of one's courage. It was unheated and so cold that we could see the ice glistening on the walls. Instead of beds, there were two wooden planks with straw sacks for mattresses. In addition, there was a wobbly table and two chairs. The water had to be carried in a bucket from a hardly movable pump in the courtyard up the two flights of stairs. Instead of a toilet, there was only an outhouse in the courtyard for everyone's use. The farmer's wife offered to give us our meals. That was a blessing, for there were no means for cooking in our room.

The other refugees who lived there were unfriendly and rude. These were people who had come from city slums, and they did not like it that we were not their kind of people. One of these families had to pass through our room to reach theirs. Day and night they disturbed us, frequently making nasty comments. It was an extremely uncomfortable situation for us, but we did not want to admit that to ourselves and we hoped for better times. To have escaped the Soviets was alone a miracle. But I kept being plagued with worries about Ilse and my grandchildren.

A few days after our arrival there, both Gisela and I became very ill with high temperatures and terrible headaches. We lay completely apathetic on our beds and could not eat anymore. The farmer's wife was afraid and called the doctor. The woman doctor who came acted very strange. She did not examine us, nor did she take our temperature. Instead, she declared indifferently, "It is only a little cold. You will be better soon." We did not improve, however, and the farmer's wife asked us if we did not want to go to the hospital, because she was not in a position to take care of us. I agreed, and several hours later an ambulance came. Gisela had to be carried on a stretcher as she no longer had the strength to walk.

When we arrived at the hospital, it was with much difficulty that I gave all the information needed to admit us. The hospital was actually a converted school, since the original hospital had been bombed out. We had to wait in a waiting room without chairs and sat on the steps of a staircase. After a lengthy, agonizing wait, the head nurse appeared and led us up the stairs to a large room. There were about twenty-five or thirty women lying there. Two nurses were making up beds for us. Gisela threw herself on one of the beds, for she could no longer stand on her legs. I heard one woman say loudly, "Those are real refugees." She was certainly right in that!

The nurses right away took care of Gisela. She was undressed and put into bed. Unfortunately, the beds were hard and without pillows, almost intolerable with the raging headache. Soon after that, two physicians appeared, who gave us a thorough examination. My temperature was 105°, and the doctors found that we had paratyphoid. We were given many shots, knowing neither what they were for nor what was being done with us. The head nurse telephoned the farmer's wife to ask that two pillows be sent. The next day one of her workers, also a refugee, came and brought us the pillows. We must have looked awful, for when he saw us, tears rolled down his cheeks.

The two doctors came to see us several times a day. We were terribly weakened, and I was only skin and bones. Our condition worsened, and we were in and out of consciousness for several weeks.

We were told later that one day it had been recommended by the staff that we be moved to the "dying chamber" where the administration of scarce medicines was minimal. However, one doctor suggested waiting one more day, and, fortunately, that day our condition turned for the better.

The doctors took great care of us. They were both fine human beings, and so were the nurses. After a few weeks we started to improve. Now and then we even felt hunger. The hospital meals were insufficient, but the good nurse tried to find us something extra as often as she could.

One day I received incredibly good news which left me overjoyed. Through a letter from my sister Jenny, I received news from Ilse. She was living in the south of Germany, had married again, and had given birth to a little girl. Everyone was happy for us—the doctors, the nurses, and the other patients in our room.

After four weeks in the hospital, Gisela was allowed to get up. She helped the nurses here and there, visited with the patients, and made friends. But it made me shudder to think that soon we would have to go back to our rough existence and start again our fight for survival. Ten days later I had improved considerably and was able to get up. In the beginning it was very difficult; I could barely take a few steps. Within a few days, however, I was able to take short walks in the garden. Soon after that, we were released from the hospital. We had been there for six weeks during which time Christmas had come and gone.

Now it was back to our passageway room. The wife of the farmer welcomed us with the announcement that we had to take care of our own meals now, because it was too much trouble for her to cook for us. An indescribably awful time began for us now. I bought myself a small stove, but unfortunately the smoke, instead of being taken out by the chimney, was blown into our room. It was almost impossible to cook. Then I bought a small electric hotplate, but that caused me much trouble because it used too much electricity. We kept hoping for an improvement in our situation. I registered Gisela at the closest high school, which was in Geesthacht closer to Hamburg. To get there on time, she had to get up very early in the morning, walk six kilometers to the train station, ride the train for forty-five minutes, and then walk again for three kilometers. This repeated itself on the way home. Fortunately, thanks to the Americans, she was given a meal at school. Eventually, I was able to get her a used bicycle. This routine was quite dangerous for Gisela because of the criminal elements abounding on the postwar scene.

The groceries that I was able to buy with the ration card were not enough to feed us. So in the summer I would go every day into the forest for many hours, collecting berries and mushrooms. It was a nutritious and delicious addition to our meager menus.

One day I received the wonderful news from Madeleine in England that she had arranged through a friend in America that all our family be sent CARE packages—to Ilse and her family, to Irene, to Jenny, and one for Gisela and myself. It was especially important for the children, for they suffered most from malnutrition. Our CARE package, which we received once a month, contained a carton of Camel cigarettes, among other things. I was able to sell these for considerable money, though there was little to buy with it. This helped us a great deal until the German economy was stabilized and conditions began to improve.

We made the acquaintance of a very nice Baltic family, who for years had lived in a suburb of Hamburg. They had a large library and lent me books. With much interest I read books about the history of art and of the world. Our daily miseries did not overwhelm us, for there was much to be glad about. Gisela also did not let things get her down. She had made friends with several other girls, and they visited each other frequently.

I heard from Ilse that her second marriage had not gone well and had ended in divorce. With a heavy heart she had left her youngest daughter with the father, for she could not take care of four children. The two boys she had put into a children's home, and the little girl, Iris, who was now six years old, was living with a foster family. She herself had found a temporary job as a secretary on the island of Norderney. She wrote to me asking if I could come for a little while to Norderney to take care of Iris, who could not adjust to living with her foster family. When Ilse's temporary job was over, she wanted to go to Frankfurt to look for another job. Gisela would finish high school in several years, and had found a boarding house for girls so she could be closer to her school. Then I left for Norderney to take charge of little Iris.

In Hamwarde I was alone now since my mother had left to help my sister in Norderney. I was fifteen years old. My nice high school in Geesthacht was closed by the British—I didn't know why. It was very sad for me, because I liked it a lot.

I then went to a nearby tailor, who had fled from the Hamburg bombing, to see if I could work for him mending clothes. My plan was to become a "famous" designer of beautiful clothes for women. Well, after one week into this adventure, I had to leave, because I could not stand working on the filthy garments he was repairing.

I then decided to see if I could find another high school to attend and found one in Bergedorf, some distance closer to Hamburg. From Hamwarde, I walked each day the six kilometers to the train station in Geesthacht, and then had about an hour's travel by train and foot to the school. This new school was really good for me. It was designed to help kids catch up from loss of study time due to the war.

I had a wonderful teacher, a Miss Autzn, who used her own method. She taught us world literature, history and geography, into all of which she incorporated some understanding of art. What a fantastic way to teach. She made me want to learn! We were also taught English, physics and mathematics.

The headmaster and my teacher found me a place to live in Bergedorf in a halfway house for girls who had been in prison for misdemeanors, so that I could get out of our "passageway room" on the

Harmwarde farm and not have to travel so far to school. This was very unpleasant for me—the girls hated me because I was not one of them. I slept in a room with two other girls. My bed was right under a dormer window and, when it rained and snowed, they would not let me close it— I think to punish me. This situation lasted almost three years until I finally finished high school. When I counted up all my moves, I found that I had gone to thirteen schools.

In 1950 I went to Heidelberg, where, with my English language ability, I was able to get a job at the United States Army headquarters in the Office of Vehicle Registration. Mother joined me there, as did later all three of Ilse's children. After a year and a half, I went to Frankfurt where Ilse was living. She had a very good office job and found me one as the personal secretary of a previous boss of hers. He was a nice gentleman, originally from Austria, who spoke heavily accented English. Our job was to create the text for informative leaflets about life in West Germany to be dropped by aircraft over Communist East Germany. The Soviet blockade of Berlin in 1949 had been defeated by the Allied airlift to that beleaguered city, and the Cold War was getting into full swing. After several more years, during which I changed jobs several times, I found a job in London at Germania Travel and moved there in 1954.

∞∞

39. My Stay in London

In 1954 a big change took place in our lives. Ilse gave up her job in Frankfurt and moved to live with us in Heidelberg, where she worked at home writing novels. Gisela moved to London, where she had found a job in a travel agency. Now that Ilse could take care of the children, I decided to move to London and be near Gisela. I also looked forward to seeing Madeleine and her family, who lived in the country. Gisela was renting a room from a family and enjoyed her work. For me she found a position with an elderly, paralyzed lady, eighty-two years old. This was the first job I had ever had in my life. I learned many things there, especially how difficult it is to be a household employee. This would never have occurred to me on my father's large estate. It was natural to me then that all the work was done by our servants. My position with the elderly lady started as a three-week trial. Then, if all went well, we would come to an agreement over permanent employment. She had assured Gisela that I was only to take care of her personally, and that I would not be required to do any other work. But it turned out differently.

My employer lived in her own three-story house in the center of the city. In addition to taking care of her, she demanded that I clean the whole house every day from top to bottom, plus doing one room a day thoroughly. Also one of my tasks was to lift my patient in and out of the bathtub, which was beyond my strength. Then I had to do all the shopping, and many other tasks. After two weeks of this I was at the end of my strength. When it was time to extend my contract, I told the lady that the work was too much for me. She was outraged. To earn a living I immediately had to look for another job. Happily, I found one right away, so that I could continue to work and earn money without interruption.

Unfortunately, I was not doing well physically and spiritually. After all, I was sixty-two and still in a weakened condition from the war and its aftermath. I desperately needed a rest. I now worked as a helper for a very nice Scottish woman, who had an eight-year-old son, named Christopher. The three of us became good friends, and we led a happy life, in spite of all the work. The house that we had to take care of and keep clean was five stories tall. I had a little room on the fifth floor, directly under the roof, with only a small dormer window. The toilet was on the fourth floor and the bath on the first. Among my tasks was the cleaning up of several offices and a few rooms rented to bachelors. According to the English custom, I would bring them tea in bed at seven in the morning, and coffee at eight o'clock. This situation seemed very strange to me, and I often had to keep myself from laughing.

After some time I noticed that I could not tolerate the constant climbing of stairs. My heart was becoming weaker and was giving me trouble. I did not want to pay attention to it, so I would grit my teeth and continue my work. Several months later, however, I felt a catastrophe nearing, and I went to see a doctor. He found my heart to be in miserable condition and ordered me to stop working. But I could not just drop my work and leave my good Scottish friend in the lurch. She could not do all that work by herself. I thus stayed another three weeks, until a replacement could be found.

In the meantime, Gisela found an apartment for the two of us, two rooms with bath and the use of a kitchen. The apartment was conveniently located so that Gisela could easily reach the subway that took her to work. It was my task now to regain my strength. Although it took a long time, I slowly improved. The doctor helped me with medication and tonics, but he insisted that I not work again. The small trust income from the English friend of my family was reinstated just at the right time to help me out. The British government also paid me a lump sum settlement on that part "frozen" during the war, on the grounds that I was a refugee from the Baltics, forced to flee to Germany to escape political persecution, and thus not a former enemy (German) alien.

I often went to visit the wonderful art galleries, the museums, and historical sights of London. I took long walks through Green Park and Hyde Park, and watched the changing of the guard at Buckingham Palace and the preparations of the Queen's mounted Life Guards. As I watched those young men on their beautiful horses, my mind drifted back forty years to the time when Macki and Mori had served in St. Petersburg in the Life Guards (Dragoons) of the German-born Tsarina, as had many sons of the Baltic German nobility.

One day as I passed by Buckingham Palace, there was a large crowd of people waiting for the Queen to drive out of the courtyard. I decided to wait with the crowd and, since it took a long time, I sat down on some steps. When the Queen appeared I stood up, but all I saw was a waving hand, for she was riding in a closed limousine. Since it was getting late, I went right away home, crossing Green Park. Halfway home I realized with dismay that I had left my handbag on the steps by Buckingham Palace. In it I had my money, my passport, and other important papers. I turned around and ran back, convinced that I would not find it anymore. When I arrived on the large square before the Palace, most people had left already, but from afar I could see my purse on the empty steps. This was wonderful, not only to find my purse again, but to see the basic honesty and decency of the English people.

Of Gisela I did not see much. She worked all day, and in the evening she was often invited out. But it was a great joy for me that my sister Irene and her two daughters also lived in London. We often visited each other and read at those times the anthroposophical writings of Rudolf Steiner. I had found no time to read and study his works since I had been a young woman. Now I started again, and found that spiritually I was much more mature. Irene lent me books, and I began to delve more and more into the spiritual science. I also loved living in London. It was a large, international city, but also very English and conservative. The beloved royal family played a large role in the daily lives of the Londoners.

One day Gisela told me that she had met an American Navy officer at a party at mutual friends of theirs. They were going out together frequently, and I looked forward to meeting him. I now had a little more money to live on and, almost for the first time in my adult life, I began to feel more optimistic about the future. Was it possible that, after years of war and deprivation, our lives had reached a turning point, and that God, with His all-embracing arms, was at last lifting us up from the abyss?

40. Gisela's Additional Commentary

My husband George and I were married in London in 1956. During the subsequent years we visited many of the former estates of my ancestors and got to know some of my German and English cousins who told us stories which filled in for me areas of family history that I had never known or had forgotten.

In 1974, we revisited England for the first time since our marriage, and there we met my cousin, Dunstan Montagu-Scott, and his wife, Patricia. Born in 1911, the youngest of Aunt Madeleine's two sons, Dunstan and his older brother Michael, were noble English gentleman in the very best sense of the word. I had met Michael, who was an accomplished portrait painter, in the 1950s. Dunstan, almost totally blind from birth, could barely read with the help of a monocle. He was plump, had thinning, white-grey hair, pink cheeks and blue eyes. He had a scintillating, infectious sense of humor and always seemed to see the vial of life as half full rather than half empty. He proudly told George and me that he had been captain of his rowing team as an undergraduate at Oxford and that they had won the championship every year he was there.

He and George hit it off at first sight. He said to George in a humorous, conspiratorial manner, "I am so glad to have discovered my colonial cousin [by marriage]. We must stick together to fend off the Krauts!" (I took that to mean me and his other Baltic German relatives.) He worked hard in his legal profession, in spite of his handicap, and we never heard him complain about his disability, which had kept him out of active military service in World War II. It may have been a blessing to him emotionally that he did not have to actively participate in the war, even though he and Aunt Madeleine hated the Nazis and their threat to England, as his grandparents and other Baltic German relatives (like me) were dodging Allied bombs and might not survive.

Dunstan told us about one particularly hilarious trip of the many he had made to Berlin during the twenties and thirties to visit our grandparents and his other relatives there. It was 1932 and he was traveling by rail from London to Berlin. He met a group of German men on the train who had been POWs in England during World War I. They complimented Dunstan on how well they had been treated and then began a round of toasts to England and Germany. By the time they arrived in Berlin, Dunstan said he was "feeling no pain" and rushed out onto the platform and into the arms of what he thought was his grandmother (Amama) but turned out to be a complete stranger. When he finally found Amama and our grandfather (Apapa) who were meeting him at the station, she, in her imperial manner, was quite disgusted and only gave him her hand to kiss, while Apapa, with a hug, was quite amused and congratulated him on "upholding the men in the family's tradition of good fun and conviviality."

Dunstan said that during his first evening with them, Amama, who knew nothing about politics, commented, "There is a wonderful man now in Germany named Adolf Hitler." "Poor dear," he continued, "she of course could not know what grief he would bring to the world that would put all our family in danger."

Invited to their charming cottage near Ashford in Kent for one weekend that fall of 1974, we were warmly greeted by Patricia, who was equally cheerful and personable. The cottage was surrounded by a beautiful rose garden and that lush countryside that is so special to England. The inside of the house was warm and hospitable.

The day after our arrival, Dunstan and Patricia announced to us that the Gypsy King of England and his wife were coming for dinner that evening. Dunstan was their legal representative. Thought to have originated in northern India in the 10th century, Gypsies first reached the British Isles in the early 16th century. The Gypsies, or Romanies, are a nomadic race, traveling the countryside, and some have even alleged that their "wanderlust" is a product of genetic determinants. At any rate, their caravan travels around Great Britain sometimes caused social, economic and political tensions. Dunstan was the very best person to represent them because he was genuinely interested in their well-being.

The King was fairly short with a stocky build, ruddy face, large nose, and red hair. He spoke with a strong cockney accent. His wife was also redheaded, but petite and quite attractive looking. After dinner, she offered to "read" our hands and "tell our fortunes." She first looked at my hand and said only that I would have a long life. When she "read" George's hand, and before making any pronouncement, she abruptly said that she was tired and could not go on with the readings. It was only later in the middle of our trip, when we received news that George's father had died suddenly and we had to rush home, that we thought back on this evening. Was it a coincidence, or can some Gypsies really see into the future?

We spent about two weeks altogether in London, Mamutschka joining us during the last week. From London, we flew to Cologne and rented a car for the drive east to Bad Berleburg to visit Aunt Jenny. On the way we passed through a village—George was undoubtedly driving too fast—and soon we noticed a Volkswagen behind us with two men, one with his hand held up waving what looked like a lollypop.

"Honey, does Polizei *mean what I think it does? It's written on the top of the car," asked George.*

"Yes. It's the police," I responded.

"O.K.," George said to me and mother. "Now here's the plan. When I pull over and he comes to the window, let's all pretend that we do not speak German (and George did not) and just smile at him and raise our hands in puzzlement as if we don't understand a word he's saying. Hopefully, as we are sort of in the middle of nowhere, they cannot speak English."

Sure enough, the policeman came to the driver's side window and started yelling at George in German. This went on for what was probably only a few seconds but seemed like forever, when Mamutschka leaned over from the back seat, tapped George on the shoulder and said, "He is saying that you were speeding through his village and that if you would pay the eighteen mark fine, he will let us go." And we did. Mother was just too honest to let that charade go on any longer.

After one night at a guest house near Aunt Jenny, George was called to the telephone early the next morning with the news from his sister that his father had died. Mother stayed on with Jenny, but we, of course, returned home immediately on the first available flight from Frankfurt.

George and I were on a Royal Viking cruise of Baltic ports with his sister and brother-in-law in July, 1987, when we docked at St. Petersburg for two days of sightseeing. There was an American history professor aboard who would lecture to us about the history of the different ports-of-call and countries we were to visit. The morning of our second day in St. Petersburg, he introduced a Russian professor from the local university, who excitedly proceeded to tell us that General Secretary Gorbachev had just announced that the Communist system was not working and that the country must push forward with "perestroika" (restructuring) and "glasnost" (openness) to provide the Soviet people with a better standard of living, and to compete on the world scene. The rest, as they say, is history.

When I think back on these and subsequent world changing events—the disintegration of the Soviet Union, the breakaway to freedom of the Baltic nations, the reunification of Germany, and the breakdown of the Communist regimes in the former Eastern Bloc countries of Europe and their renaissance as democracies—indeed, the end of the

Cold War and the "Evil Empire"—I thank God that President Reagan and Gorbachev were in power at the same time. After all, when Reagan was speaking in front of the Berlin Wall in 1987, he had the guts to exclaim, "Mr. Gorbachev, tear down this wall!"—and Gorbachev had the guts to let it happen, regardless of the consequences. When I hear Americans gloat and say, "We won the Cold War," I think how shortsighted that statement really is. We all were victors in the Cold War, because their economic and political revival in relative freedom enhanced America's national security and hopefully is providing a better life for all those humans in the East who have struggled so long and hard to achieve it.

In 1989 we decided to attend the family reunion of my von Samson-Himmelstjerna (Mamutschka's maiden name) relatives, which was to be held in late May at Castle (Schloss) Höhnscheid in the country just west of Kassel, roughly in the middle of now reunified Germany.

As we approached Castle Höhnscheid by car, we saw a large, country baroque structure painted orange-yellow with white-trimmed windows. I immediately noticed that the family colors were flying on the top of the building. We learned later that the castle was once a monastery and thus, with its many bedrooms with bath for the monks, suited itself well for a large family reunion.

After settling into our room and freshening up, we went to the front steps of the castle, where a small group had gathered to enjoy the view and mild early evening. There were spectacular fields of "rape" in the distance, a plant with large yellow flowers which is sometimes used as fodder and whose crushed seeds yield a good cooking oil.

I had never met any of my cousins who were attending the reunion. After introductions, George passed around a gigantic bottle of Johnny Walker Black Label scotch which he had bought duty-free at the airport. What we perceived as a rather stiff, German reception of us in the beginning, soon evolved into a warm embrace.

In this setting soon a tall, gangly, gregarious cousin came up to us and with a big smile said, "Hi! I'm Hasso Samson from South Ca'lina." My third cousin, about seven years younger, Hasso had been in a student exchange program in the early 1950s and spent a year as a senior in high school with a South Carolina family. George and I had gotten to know his older brother Dieter and wife Hella [née von Dehn] when they lived in Washington, D.C. He was an agronomist with the World Bank. Now retired, they live in Germany and Spain.

Hasso, now also recently retired, was then an official in the German government. He can speak British English, American English or South Ca'lina whatever, and is also fluent in French, Dutch, Spanish and Italian. While he was still working, he would travel to the States quite often with his boss to visit their counterparts in the U.S. government in Washington. During these trips he would almost always visit his "mom" in South Carolina, who is apparently in her nineties, and then tie in a visit with George and me in North Carolina.

The next day Hasso's wife Heilke [née von Stakelberg] took us on a tour of nearby sights. I mention the maiden names of these ladies because they are all of Baltic German nobility. In other words, for the most part Balts married Balts. George jokingly said to me later that evidently he was the only "commoner" at the reunion. While it was evident that part of the cohesiveness of this family and of all Baltic German families was their nostalgia for their Baltic homeland and estates of their forebears, they were firmly footed in the world of today, where what you make of yourself is what counts.

Mamutschka sometimes talked to us about attitudes among the Baltic German nobility. Theirs was a code of honor and behavior going back to the Crusaders and the Baltic Teutonic Knights, who tried to follow the teachings of Christ. However, true nobility of character, she used to say, was a state of mind, an attitude, an ideal available to all human beings who, being human, have a mixed record in achieving it. This nobility of the human spirit, in the final analysis, does not exist from the decree of any monarch or, she laughingly said, can it be bestowed just because you might have a crown sewn on your underwear.

The last evening at the reunion was special. After a fairly late, celebratory dinner with everyone dressed formally, the sound of waltz music resounded near the wide hallway that was lined with medieval armor. Soon, almost everyone was waltzing in the dim light, the music provided by a tape player. This continued to almost midnight when we entered the dining room to partake of ice cold vodka in small shot glasses, accompanied by delicious black bread with a kind of heavy lard spread on it. There were many toasts to everyone's health ("prosit" in German). A very nice cousin, retired from the German Navy and fluent in English, offered to stay with George and translate when needed.

"In the old days when we could afford it," he told George, "this would have been bread with caviar. But drink up and eat up, for you will not get drunk with this fare." And they did and they didn't. George said later he had fully expected some of the gentlemen to smash their glasses into the fireplace (as he had seen in the movies), but of course that would not happen—there were ladies present. Soon the music changed to jazz, swing and Latin tempos. The young couples of the family led the way as we all transitioned to today, and George and I felt more in our element.

The next morning, church services were held in the castle chapel. We were so impressed with the college-age children of the cousins who organized and presented the service. It was all in German, but I summarized it for George later. We sang those great Christian hymns "A Mighty Fortress is Our God" and "Onward Christian Soldiers," George singing in English as hard as he could, and everyone else, of course, in German. It was one of those special moments when I think we all were conscious of what bound our diverse cultures together, our common Christian heritage enveloping us all.

The next day before we left, we talked to Hasso for a while. The conversation turned to some events of World War II that he remembered. He told us that, as the Russians approached from the east, his father, who was the lands manager for the Duke of Saxony, brought his family from Silesia east of Dresden to seek shelter in the Duke's castle on the Elbe just upriver and south of the city of Dresden. Hasso, then seven, said he remembered clearly the nights of February 13-15, 1945, when Allied bombers destroyed this beautiful baroque city, killing more than 25,000 people, many of them refugees from the east. Hasso said they could see the bombing from the castle and smell the scent of death and destruction for days. Of course, Mamutschka and I were taking the same beating in Berlin.

George and I were in Berlin and Dresden in the fall of 2005 on a mini-reunion tour with a few of his Princeton classmates. We are happy to report that many of the beautiful baroque buildings and churches of Dresden have been rebuilt, an enormous project begun under the Soviets and East Germans and now being financed by donations from all over the world.

I had not returned to my Baltic homeland since we had left Latvia in 1939 on a German refugee ship, just after the war had started and just before the Soviet Union's occupation of that area and half of Poland, as agreed to in the Hitler-Stalin Pact of August, 1939. Early in 1994, I received notice that the von zur Mühlens were going to have a mini-reunion in Tallinn [historical German name: Reval], Estonia, and that many activities were planned, including visits to many of the Baltic

German manor houses on the former estates. George, our daughter Toby and I decided to go and join the thirty or so other family members, spouses, grown children and significant others, as they now say. We were to spend about ten days in Estonia and Latvia, seven days in Berlin, and then finish our trip in Exeter, England, where Patricia and Dunstan lived in his retirement close to their two daughters and their families.

The activities and Estonian itinerary were planned by my twin second cousins Max and Bengt Mühlen, who live in Berlin. Bengt and his wife Irmgard, as I have previously written, founded Chronos Films, where, through the years, they have produced many world-class documentaries about the rise of the Nazis, the Hitler period, the Holocaust and World War II, etc. Other than Max, Bengt and Irmgard, and Heinz and Putti Mühlen from Munich, whom George and I had all met previously, we really knew none of the other family members, with the exception of Patrik Mühlen, the family historian who lives in Bonn.

When George and I—Toby was arriving a week later—left from Raleigh-Durham Airport for our connection through New York and Frankfurt to Tallinn, the curbside check-in porter unfortunately attached the tag for Tallahassee, Florida, instead of Tallinn, to my bag only. Fortunately, I had a carry-on with a change of clothing. It took a week for the airline to trace my luggage and get it to Tallinn—and would have probably taken longer if it hadn't been for Toby, who was a travel agent in Nashville, Tennessee, had prepared our tickets, and knew just the right person to contact.

The first few days were spent touring the beautiful city of Tallinn and getting to know all those cousins. One day we visited the Dom (cathedral) on the hill in Old Town. As we walked around the nave of the cathedral, looking at the lacquered, wooden plaques mounted on the walls under the high windows bearing the coats-of-arms of many of the families of the Baltic German nobility (my father's family plaque was on the floor being repaired), we came upon a large, marble sepulcher. It has an inscription in Latin which reads roughly as follows:

"Here lie the remains of Samuel Gregory, Scotsman, who served bravely as a general in the service of Catherine the Great."

George, whose North Carolina maternal grandfather was also named Samuel Gregory, turned to me and said,

"You see, Gisela. Our ancestors may have fought together in the service of Catherine the Great. You and I were destined to be here together at this time and place."

And as we spoke, the exalted sound of the organ drifted throughout the church, and we felt there was something special taking place that was calling to us from ages past.

We also visited some of the old commercial buildings of my Mühlen forefathers affiliated with the Hanseatic League, a monopolistic, trading confederation of merchants originating in Lübeck, Germany in the 12th century and later including most all of the Baltic ports, as well as Hamburg and London, to name a few.

After a few days, we left early one morning on an all-day bus tour about 100 miles southeast to Tartu [historical German name: Dorpat], the old university town where my father went to school. After briefly stopping at some of the beautiful manor houses of other Baltic families, we arrived at the ruins of Eigstfer, the estate of Uncle Victor, my father's oldest brother. There was not much to see except the brick foundation of a large structure. Our next stop, which I had much anticipated, was my father's birthplace, Woiseck, located in the middle of present-day Estonia. It had encompassed almost 50,000 acres before the expropriation. The large but unassuming old house was without the glass entrance veranda that Mother had described in her memoirs and which apparently had been torn off sometime in the intervening years. It was now an insane asylum. We met the Estonian doctor who very kindly showed us around the large, high-ceilinged reception rooms, but we could not visit the rest of the house because of the patients.

We arrived in Tartu around noon and picked up a nice, elderly Estonian lady fluent in German to help us as a guide and interpreter. After lunch, we spent a few hours touring the old university and a local cemetery. No one of my immediate family was buried there, as my father died in 1946 in a Soviet prisoner of war camp in Russia, and my mother's mother died in Potsdam in 1945, and her father in England in 1950, where he was then living with Aunt Madeleine. Papi's mother and father died in Germany in 1942. On our way back to Tallinn, we stopped for supper at a charming little restaurant on the main road that was a converted windmill.

In retrospect, two of the next few days were for me a waste of time. It was quite hot that year for late July in the Baltics (and later in

Berlin), so Max and Bengt had planned a bus trip to a nearby village, where we took a ferry to one of the little islands close to Tallinn. There was absolutely nothing to do or see there, but George, forever loving the sea, could not pass up a dip in the Gulf of Finland (he had to change in the bushes). Later he said, "What a stupid thing for me to do. No telling what the Russians left buried in that water which might contaminate the area!" [Estonia regained its independence from the Soviet Union only in 1991.]

After lunch at the Yacht Club the next day, a few of us, under Max and Bengt's leadership (I think Irmgard and Toby were smart enough not to go), had rented a small sailboat for the afternoon to have a leisurely sail around Tallinn harbor. It was extremely hot and there was very little wind. The whole idea pleased George immensely as he recalled his childhood sailing days in North Carolina.

Somehow, without a motor, we managed to get out into the middle of the harbor, and then the wind completely died away. The young people were sunning themselves and having a great time, and Max and Bengt, both PhDs, were philosophizing, alternately in German and English. After enough of this, George and I started talking in English with the Russian skipper of the boat, whose name was Alexei. He was very personable and friendly and proceeded to tell us a most interesting story about the plight of the immigrant Russians in Estonia. [The Soviet occupation lasted from 1940 until 1991. The last troops of the new Russian Confederation left in August 1994 and Estonia joined NATO and the European Union in 2004.]

"During the Soviet era, hundreds of thousands of Russian-speaking migrants, mostly from Ukraine, were relocated by the Communists to this country, sometimes against their will. I was one of those. When Estonia regained her independence, Estonians were in the majority, but not by much. There was a backlash against Russians who were not born here. My children are citizens, but Russian immigrants like me are denied citizenship and thus much of our civil rights." [By 2005, Russians who had immigrated were down to about 25 percent of the 1.3 million population. Feeling less threatened and under the NATO "umbrella," Estonians have hopefully improved in their treatment of Russians.]

"Are your parents living?" I asked.

"My elderly mother lives in the Crimea." He, of course, knew of our Baltic German background and why we were in Tallinn.

"Alexei, then you and I have something in common, don't we? Our countrymen have both been thrown out of the Baltics, albeit for different reasons. Let's hope that with the end of the Cold War the future will be brighter."

"Yes, let's drink to that," he said with a big smile. And he, George and I clinked ours glasses of Coca-Cola together as the wind picked up for our return to land.

We had rented a car at the beginning of our stay in Tallinn, and so the next day George, Toby and I retraced the bus trip to Tartu with the intent of finding Hummelshof, which we had reason to believe was now called "Hummuli." It was shown on the map of Estonia to be about forty miles southwest of Tartu near the Latvian border. Thanks to the training from his father and the United States Navy, George can find anything, and did! We stopped in Tartu to pick up the same nice, Estonian guide and interpreter, fluent in German—but not English—as I do not understand or speak Estonian.

As we approached the small village of Hummuli, I glimpsed the tall tower through the trees in the distance, and as we pulled closer I recognized the old brick house from a photo at home "circa 1912." I learned later that a few of the village houses were the original ones where some of the estate workers had lived in my grandparents' time. Apparently, the village and surrounding thousands of acres had been part of the estate.

"This is it," said George. I was speechless. We pulled into the long driveway and jumped out of the car at the front door. The door was unlocked, and with our guide in tow, we literally rushed into the house. In the foyer a man was working and looked at us in a surprised but not unfriendly manner. The guide proceeded to tell him that I was a descendant of the original owners.

"I am a general contractor," he told her in Estonian. "We are turning this mansion into a private boarding school. I am going to get the mayor of Hummuli, as I know he would like to meet all of you."

In a few minutes, the two of them returned and the mayor greeted me in good German, at first bowing formally—I almost hugged him. They were all so friendly—not a trace of the old but understandable resentments against the Baltic German ruling class—and they loved

America and Americans. As Mother had written, this estate had been sold to Count Frederic Berg in 1912, whose coat of arms was in one of the rooms, and my family moved to Peddeln in 1914. When the expropriation took place right after the Russian Revolution and the Baltic countries' independence, the authorities had offered to let my grandfather Axel keep his Peddeln estate with all its land, because he was so beloved in the area and also headed the Baltic Red Cross. But he refused because he could not accept treatment superior to his fellow Balts; so he and Amama moved to Germany with the whole family (with the exception of my mother, who had just married my father in Riga), as did most of his contemporaries.

We toured the whole house and found it much as Mamutschka had described it in her memoirs, including the same parquet floors and steps to the tower where she had studied and daydreamed early in the mornings, while contemplating that wonderful view of nature. Afterwards, the mayor invited George and me over to his cottage, just a short walk away, which had a lovely rose garden, while Toby explored what used to be the English park to the rear of the house. She went clear to the river, about a half mile. Although mostly overgrown, there was still a trace of the beautiful trees and plants not usually seen in the Baltics that Apapa had picked up in different countries on his many travels abroad. When she returned, the three of us left to return our guide to Tartu and then to make the two-hour drive back to Tallinn.

The next evening we had our final family dinner and goodbyes. Everybody liked Toby and George—Toby had studied German at *boarding school and could speak and understand a little. Poor George had struggled so hard to learn some German, but one day a few years earlier he had thrown up his hands and said, "I can't learn a language that has three 'thes'—*der, die *and* das, *with no apparent clue for the most part as to which one goes with which noun. I'm too old to just memorize it. You'll just have to put up with me saying, 'What did they say? What did they say?'"*

The next day we left early for our motor trip to Latvia. We planned to find Peddeln, just over the Estonian-Latvian border and on our map printed as "Pedele," a slightly different Latvian word, and then to end up in Riga for two nights, where we also were going to look for nearby Planup, my birthplace in 1931. We did not know whether either country house had been destroyed during the war. The whole distance from Tallinn to Riga by this route is about 240 miles.

It should be pointed out that, in my grandparents' day, before the Revolution, there was no border between present day Estonia and Latvia—the province was called "Livonia," a part of Czarist Russia, and thus both Hummelshof and Peddeln were in the same province. The area was split between the two countries at the end of World War I.

As we came to the border crossing and handed over our passports to the Latvians, I thought I noticed a definite change in the atmosphere—not nearly as friendly as the reception we had just received from the Estonians. But a little sullenly they finally stamped our passports and waved us through.

George had figured out from his map that we should take the first right off the main paved highway, which was also a paved narrower road. After a short drive, the asphalted road turned into gravel, and we slowed to look both ways. Fairly soon, on the right, I noticed a large mansion at the end of a long dirt entrance road. I could see the French chateau style of the house with its mansard roof. We did not have a photograph, only Mamutschka's description in her memoirs.

"That has to be it," exclaimed George. We drove to the front of the house and saw from one of the upper windows a soldier standing with a girl, looking out at us; they did not look very friendly. George thought his uniform looked Russian, and we knew for a fact that the Russian Confederation had not completed their withdrawal from the Baltics. Soon a young adult girl came out of the house. Fortunately, she spoke German, as I had long forgotten the Latvian I had learned as a child.

I didn't know whether she was Latvian or Russian but proceeded to tell her that my grandfather had built the house years ago, without giving her too much information on the specifics—the expropriation of lands from the Baltic Germans, etc. She immediately started giving me a run-down of the repairs needed for the house: the roof leaked, the inside walls were cracking, the water well had become too old and unreliable, and a few other problems. Although I was anxious to see the inside of the house, I was also a little uneasy about the whole scene. I translated for George, and he said, "I don't like the way this smells. They could shoot us and probably nobody would ever find us. No one else knows where we are. Let's get out of here before she tries to give the place back to you and then demands all the repairs!" With that, we quickly took a few pictures and jumped into the car and left. After another hundred miles, we arrived in Riga at dusk.

Our hotel was right in the center of the city, reasonably comfortable but overpriced. The next morning, George wanted to rest a bit after breakfast, so Toby and I booked a half-day sightseeing tour by bus. Riga is a beautiful old city and, like Tallinn, had very little war damage. That afternoon we explored with George the shopping and commercial area near our hotel and ended up at the Riga Cathedral, where I knew there was a stained glass window depicting my ancestor, Hermann Samson, greeting King Gustav II Adolph to Riga in 1621, thereby avoiding the destruction of the city.

We rang the bell at the front entranceway and fairly soon a lady came to the door and peeked out. "May we come in and see the cathedral?" I asked.

"No! Cathedral is closed!" I then explained that we were from America, had to leave the next day and the particulars of our interest.

"No. Cathedral is closed for the next few days." She then actually closed the door in our faces. There was no appeal to a higher authority. I left with a bitter taste in my mouth, but at least we have a picture of the stained glass window scene on the wall in our Durham home. Hopefully, in the intervening years, most Latvians have become friendlier to foreign tourists, including Baltic Germans like me wishing to visit their old homeland.

The next morning we left fairly early to retrace, for about twenty-five miles, the main four-lane highway toward Estonia to where George had found "Planupe" printed on the map. Our task was much more difficult, as I believed Planup was further off the main road than the other family estates we had seen. It was our plan, after hopefully finding my birthplace, to cut across the countryside to the Gulf of Riga, without returning to Riga, and then drive due north along the coast to Pärnu [historical German name: Pernau], a lovely seaside Estonian resort where we could have supper. The total distance to Tallinn by this direct route was around 170 miles.

We turned off the main road at what we thought was the right place, and sure enough, we soon saw a passenger-bus stop on the paved service road with a name that we had previously associated with Planup. We turned left onto the service road and, after a short drive, turned right onto a single-vehicle dirt road. We rode deeper and deeper into the forest without finding any sign of the old country house.

"I am sure these woods were a part of the Planup estate before the expropriation," said George, "but I think we should turn back to the service road because, again, we don't know if the 'natives' are friendly."

We turned around and drove back to the service road, all this time not seeing any sign of a human being. We reached the bus stop and short connector road to the main highway and noticed that the service road went on a little further in the other direction past the connector road. We drove on and then saw a dirt road on the left leading to what looked like a small farm house. There was a car in the yard, and two men were standing outside. "Let's drive in here and see if those men can help us find Planup," said George. When we got out of the car, we found that one of the men spoke fairly good English. I introduced us and explained to him that we were looking for my birthplace.

"Well, this is Planup!" he exclaimed. "I bought it last year from the State," he added somewhat suspiciously—I think he thought for a moment we were in Latvia to try to claim it back. We were standing by a small wooden cabin and noticed close-by the ruins of the main house, with everything destroyed except some of the floor at the ground level.

"I recently built this cabin over the foundation of another destroyed section attached to the main house and use it as a weekend retreat from Riga. I am in the computer business there and have traveled to the west coast of the States several times for training."

"Yes, that was used by my parents as a guesthouse. May we walk over and have a closer look at the main house ruins?"

"Why, of course. Please look around as much as you wish." He was beginning to sound almost friendly.

We all walked over to about the middle of what used to be the side of the house when I saw something that made my heart leap.

"Look, do you see that light blue and white floor tile? That was my mother's bathroom!" Suddenly, all those happy memories of Planup as a child—both before and after my parents were divorced—came rushing into my head, and I was both overjoyed by this moment but then deeply saddened as I remembered some of the mental pain and suffering that my mother had experienced over the years and finally the terrible

218

and unjustified execution of my father by the Soviets in 1946. Whatever dreams they had in their youth to raise a family and to live a happy and productive life together at Planup were just not meant to be.

We walked completely around the ruins, and I pointed out to everybody where various things had been located as best I could from my memory as a seven-year-old child. It was quite hot and there were lots of insects flying around and nipping at us, so, after about an hour's visit, we thanked the new owner of Planup for showing us the property, wished him well, and left. We arrived back in Tallinn after a nice drive up the coast of the Gulf of Riga with a stopover for supper at Pärnu.

The next day we flew to Berlin via Frankfurt to change flights. We had rented a car at Tegel Airport and drove into the city to locate a small, less expensive hotel that George had picked out from his "research" on cheaper Berlin hotels in "uptown" locations. The hotel was on the Friedrichstrasse, on the east side of the Brandenburg Gate, and a few blocks south of the avenue Unter den Linden. Only five years before, this area was still part of East Berlin and the German Democratic Republic.

The hotel was awful! It reminded Toby of a youth hostel, with lots of noisy young people running around. We were too old for that! There were no amenities. Furthermore, it was the first few days of August and unseasonably hot, just as it had been in the Baltics, and there was no air conditioning. After one miserable night there, Toby located a fairly new Hilton hotel with air conditioning just around the corner and was able, with her travel agent ID, to book us two rooms for the rest of our stay in Berlin at very reasonable rates.

One of our goals while we were in Berlin was to drive to Potsdam, see the Sanssouci (French for "without care") summer palace of Frederick the Great, and to also try to find the villa where my grandparents had lived with all the family during the 1920s. All we had to go by was a photograph of the villa with my grandparents standing at the entranceway and my mother's description in her memoirs that it was "across the street from the park entrance to Sanssouci." I remembered having it pointed out to me when we were living in Potsdam at the end of the war and recalled that the Soviets had made it one of their headquarters. At that time there was a large poster picture of Stalin hanging over the entranceway, with similar pictures on either side of Lenin and General Georgi Zhukov, the commanding Soviet general in the battle for Berlin.

After visiting the palace, we drove around the park and soon reached a street with houses facing the park. All of a sudden, we recognized the villa from the photo. There was a high metal fence separating it from the street, with a plaque on it saying that it was a school. As it was Sunday, the entrance gate was padlocked and so we could not go in. Sure enough, on the left side of the villa the Soviets had added the ugly-looking concrete sentry box typical of a headquarters building at that time.

In the fall of 1999 George and I flew to London with the intent of having a long talk with my cousin Nanusch von der Osten-Sacken about family history. Our plan was to then take the chunnel train under the English Channel to Paris, where we would spend a few days, and afterwards travel around Normandy for several days more.

Born in 1913, Nanusch was eighty-six at the time we were there and had lived in England since the late 1940s with her mother and sister, both of whom were now deceased. She had once been an accomplished painter and had done the portrait of Mother which hangs in our home. Petite, witty and full of stories, she lived in a retirement apartment building in the north of London where she had arranged for George and me to rent an unoccupied room with bath. We had a series of talks over several days, which are summarized as follows:

"Mother," I reminded her, "had written that Apapa had bought two villas in mid-1918 in Cannstatt, so that Amama and the rest of the family would be safe from the turmoil in the Baltics, and also so she could be near her sister and enjoy life at the Court of King William II of Württemberg. Of course, 'the rest of the family' did not include Madeleine, who lived in London with her husband, Ralph Montagu-Scott, nor Mother, who, with Papi, was struggling to survive in Latvia, and then you and your family were still in Riga, where your father later worked a while for the Russians as an architect. Is that right?"

"Yes, that is all true. Apapa went back and forth between Cannstatt and the Baltics to check on the situation there, and later he,

Uncle Paul [von Stryk] and Rembert joined the Landeswehr *[group of Baltic Germans formed to fight the Red Army], which had allied with the Russian White Army to fight the Bolsheviks. Early in 1919, after the old king had abdicated, he bought the villa in Potsdam so that he could be closer to his business interests in Berlin, and the family moved there. My immediate family left Latvia a while later to live in the Potsdam villa. Apapa was determined to support his whole family until things settled down in Germany and we could fend for ourselves. And that took quite a while. In the early 1920s we were like a menagerie. Besides us and Gabie, Rembert and Jenny, Wilhem von Cramer, whom Jenny married about this time, also came to live there. We didn't like him."*

"Neither did I. He and Jenny lived near mother and me in Eggersdorf in the 1940s. He was a jerk."

"He didn't do anything to earn a living; just puttered around the villa's garden a bit. Breakfast was served promptly at 8:00 in the morning, but he would appear at 10:00 wanting his full breakfast. Apapa gave him an allowance of 400 pounds a month, which was a lot in those days. I had a school friend who observed all of this activity at the villa and she said to me one day, 'I wish I were in your family. Mine is so dull in comparison.'

"In 1925 I was sent to finishing school in Stuttgart for five years and Ljuba followed me there soon after. When I graduated, I enrolled in the Art Academy, but later in the 1930s I needed to look for work, but what could I do? None of us were trained to do anything! I tried to learn typing—to no avail. Our grandparents had moved to their beautiful,

spacious apartment in Berlin in 1932 and so mother, Ljuba and I were living there; the others had scattered elsewhere. I remember once getting a modeling job—by then I was about twenty—and they told us to smile, smile, and smile as we showed our wares. Nowadays they look so grim!"

"Tell us about Madeleine and Ralph. You know Apapa would travel somewhere in the world about every four years to get away from life on the estates and to see what was going on in the world. I came across a journal he had written in 1912 when he traveled with a group of Balts to America and then to Jamaica and Panama. Evidently, according to the journal, Ralph and Madeleine went with him."

"Well, I was not born until 1913 but I can tell you what I later heard from Madeleine and also observed. As you know, she went to finishing school in Sussex, England, and Ralph, who was ten years older, was living nearby on their estate, Ifold, with his mother. The estate consisted of a manor house set in about 120 acres of parkland and 1100 acres more of surrounding land. One day he saw Madeleine across a fence, walking in a field belonging to the school. They struck up a conversation and the rest you know. They had a big wedding at Hummelshof in 1908 and went to live at Ifold with his mother. Apparently, the mother-in-law was bad-tempered, so eventually they moved to London, where Ralph had a house first in Piccadilly and later in Hyde Park Gate.

"You know Madeleine was extremely beautiful and a femme fatale, as well as being smart and resourceful. She was a real belle on the London social scene, and I think she found Ralph rather boring.

When I met him later, I thought he was very nice. He spent much time at Ifold, raising his Irish wolfhounds. At some point she met Richard Tilden-Smith, a very wealthy British financier and industrialist who was later also a Member of Parliament. He died in 1931, but apparently during the 20s, or maybe even a little earlier, he and Madeleine started a relationship—she and Ralph must have had some sort of arrangement. She did not divorce him until much later. I remember once Madeleine visiting her parents at Potsdam with Tilden-Smith. It was in 1925 just before I left for finishing school."

"Yes, I know about Tilden-Smith from Mother. He apparently adored the whole family and set up trusts for our grandparents, Madeleine, and all the other siblings. Mother was still receiving a little income from her trust when she died in 1985."

"Well, his as well as Apapa's generosity helped them all at the time they needed it most. Gabie went to live in Nice for a while in 1928, and later she moved to an agricultural estate near Johannesburg, South Africa, where she worked as a horticulturist. I think she had a love interest there, but, as you know, she never married. In 1956, when she already had lung cancer, she went to live with Rembert and Sybil in Australia, where she died the same year. Rembert had completed his doctorate in agronomy at Heidelberg in 1928 and with Tilden-Smith's help, and a lot of hard work, he went to western Australia, near Perth, and pursued his dream of having a large sheep and wheat farm which he called 'Livonia.' That was where he met Sybil, who was English-Australian."

"*I know. When Rembert and Sybil visited us in New Bern in 1974, Sybil told us that Gabie had died in her arms. They were on one of their periodic half-year trips to Europe and spent three weeks with us and Mamutschka. That was the first and last time that George and I ever saw them. Sybil was lovely, so full of life and good humor, and very sporty. I remember one day we all went swimming in the river in front of our house, and as she made a perfect dive into the water from our dock—what a great figure she had!—George yelled one of those comments he usually saved for 'yankee' visitors, 'Hey Sybil, if you see an alligator swimming about, don't bother it because it eats the water moccasins.' Without missing a beat when her head came up from the water, she yelled back, 'Not to worry, darling. Where I come from they are <u>crocodiles</u>!' But let's get back to Madeleine.*"

"*In 1936 Madeleine came to Berlin with Dunstan to visit her parents and to attend some of the Berlin Olympics. Ljuba and I would always have a good time with Dunstan—we would go out on the town until the wee hours of the morning. I remember one night we got a little too tipsy and had trouble finding our way home to the apartment on Bayreuther Strasse.*

"*Madeleine had been in ill health for several years, which finally was diagnosed as liver trouble (and cured several years later). It was decided that I would go to England the next year to help run her household. She was always trying to find for me a British blue blood to marry—to no avail. I remember one time Dunstan and Patricia, who were now married, took me to a dance at Oxford. It was so funny; there were hardly any chaperones for the girls, but many of the boys' fathers were there to make sure their sons behaved themselves and got home on time.*

"*Time passed. It was 1939 and I was still there. In late August, several days before the war started, Madeleine took me over to some soirée on the Belgian coast at a casino and spa. On the morning of September 1ˢᵗ we woke up to the news that Germany had just invaded Poland. She immediately found a way to get us back to London before the end of the day. Early the next morning, she said to me that there was going to be a terrible war and that I had to go back to Berlin immediately. Britain and France had already given Germany an ultimatum to withdraw from Poland. I started crying and saying that I did not want to go, and Ralph very kindly tried to persuade her to let me stay. 'No, she has to go,' she said. 'It's going to be a long war, and her mother, Ljuba and my parents are going to need her. I have already found out from a friend at the Foreign Office what would happen to her if she stays here. She will be interned as an enemy alien and of no use to anyone. And guess what! They are going to put the women on the Isle of Wight just off the southern English coast and the men on the Isle of Man in the Irish Sea between England and Ireland.'*

"*When I heard her say that, I began to think of what an awful fate it would be to end up interned on an island with a bunch of German women. I then agreed to go, thinking that maybe she would be wrong about the duration of the war and it would be over in a few weeks, and I could then return to England. Late that day Dunstan and Patricia took* *me to Victoria Station, and I got on probably the last overnight boat train which would take me to Germany via Holland. We were all crying as I leaned out the window and waved goodbye, each of us wondering what our fate would be. When I arrived in Berlin on September 3rd, Britain and France were already at war with Germany as of late that morning."*

Our visit in 1999 was the last time we saw Nanusch. She died in 2005 at the age of ninety-two. What a valiant and spunky personality she was. She faced the hand that life had dealt her with her head held high.

EPILOGUE

Soon after George and I were married in 1956, Mamutschka immigrated to America and lived with us in Washington, where George worked at the Department of State until we left for Paraguay in 1959 when he was assigned to the embassy there. She eventually moved to a small apartment overlooking Rock Creek Park where she could "commune" with nature on her daily walks and also walk to the wonderful Washington Zoo. She found an Anthroposophy study group and so was able to resume her readings of the works of Rudolf Steiner. Here are excerpts from her memoirs about her life in Washington:

The years that I spent almost totally alone in Washington were most significant for my inner development. When I arrived in the States, I was spiritually ailing. I was shy with people and kept my distance. I was overly sensitive and lacked confidence. The traumatic experiences that I had had in my life had deeply shocked my inner being. The peace that surrounded me in Washington and the communion with nature that was afforded me by the nearness of the park became a healing power for my soul. Also my weekly reading group of Rudolf Steiner's writings and my studies at home had a calming and healing effect on me.

Although I lived almost entirely within myself, my world was extremely interesting and large. I was passionately involved in many things. The great philosophers Socrates and Plato delighted me with their exacting logic and their spiritually inspired wisdom. The more modern philosophers had nothing to offer me. They are great thinkers in the framework of the material world, but they are unable to overstep that limit and make contact with the spiritual. They did not interest me for that reason, for matter is nothing more than the spiritual materialized. All humans, animals, plants, minerals, etc. have a spiritual origin, and, as long as we do not recognize this, we are in error and will not get anywhere in life.

————————

My reading group dissolved after a few years, mostly due to deaths. At first I missed our weekly gatherings, but later I enjoyed the protective isolation furthered by its absence. Time went by quickly. I had divided my day into parts. In the morning I made order in the apartment and prepared my lunch, which consisted of raw vegetables, grains, nuts, cottage cheese, etc. I am a vegetarian for various reasons. The thought that an animal has to die so that I can eat its flesh is intolerable for me. . . After my chores, I studied Anthroposophy and meditated, and then I took a walk in the park. In the late afternoon and evening, I studied history, watched television, and listened to classical music on the radio. In any case, every day came quickly to an end. Frequently, I visited the

National Gallery of Art. There I went to lectures on art . . . and attended free musical concerts from time to time. . . I became more and more absorbed in the paintings.

At the age of seventy-nine, Mother took painting courses in Washington, first with watercolors and later with oils. Eventually, she concentrated on portrait painting. In 1971 she moved to an apartment we had for her in our North Carolina home. Everyone she met of our friends and relatives loved her. She painted portraits of all our children and was commissioned by some of our friends and neighbors to paint their children as well. She won a first prize blue ribbon in a local art contest with her portrait of our son. Aside from portraits, she probably painted at least a hundred other works of varying subject matter.

In 1985 Mamutschka died in New Bern at the age of ninety-two. Here is the ending narrative in her memoirs which she completed in 1973:

Truly, we have found our good fortune in the States, thanks to the generosity and freedom of this beautiful land, and thanks to the openness and friendliness of its inhabitants. I must also express a very private thank you—that I was given the chance, after all the dark storms in my life through which God's hand guided and protected me, to lead a happy, peaceful and harmonious life in my old age.

Mamutschka's example of courage in the face of adversity and her deep spirituality have been an inspiration for all of her family. She was truly a noble lady.